Famous attacks and assassinations

30 real cases

Phillips Tahuer

Ediciones Afrodita

Contents

Introduction

Throughout history, world leaders have held positions of immense power and responsibility. Still, they have also been the targets of violent conspiracies seeking to change the course of politics and society through force. Attacks and assassinations, beyond the tragic events they represent, have reflected deep tensions, ideological conflicts, and power struggles, marking turning points in the history of their nations and, in some cases, of the entire world.

This book compiles 30 real and emblematic cases of attacks and assassinations that have cut short or put the lives of important leaders in grave danger. From leaders who fell under the edge of treason, such as Julius Caesar, to those who survived against all odds, such as Ronald Reagan or Fidel Castro, these stories show how political decisions, personal rivalries, and social movements were the backdrop for these violent actions.

Each case presented in this book not only narrates the details of the assassination itself but also explores the political and social context that gave rise to it. Whether due to revolutions, civil wars, extremist ideologies, or simple vendettas, these assassinations reflect a constant in human history: dissatisfaction with the established power and the attempt to redefine the future by drastic means.

Some of these assassinations have triggered wars, while others have been used to consolidate or weaken regimes. The reasons that led to these attacks are as varied as the figures who suffered them, but they all have in common the search for radical change, often regardless of the cost.

In this journey through some of the darkest episodes in political history, the acts themselves are revealed and the hidden forces that drove them, demonstrating how the fate of leaders and nations have often been inextricably linked.

1. The Assassination of Julius Caesar: The End of the Roman Republic

The assassination of Julius Caesar, which occurred on March 15, 44 BC, is one of the most famous episodes in ancient history. This assassination not only ended the life of one of Rome's most influential leaders but also sealed the fate of the Roman Republic, giving way to the Empire.

To understand the assassination of Julius Caesar, it is crucial to place it within a prolonged crisis that the Roman Republic was experiencing in the first century BC. During this period, Rome was experiencing extreme political tensions. Military expansion had led Rome to become a superpower, but this growth also exacerbated economic inequality and increased corruption within the government. The senatorial class, which ruled Rome, was divided into two large factions: the populares, who supported reforms that benefited the lower classes and sought greater control of the popular leaders, and the optimates, defenders of the traditional aristocratic power of the Senate.

Julius Caesar allied himself with the populares, who promoted reforms that limited the power of the Senate and favored the plebs. Throughout his career, Caesar rose rapidly, largely due to his charisma, political skill, and military victories, especially during the conquest of Gaul (58–50 BC). However, his ambitions brought him into confrontation with the optimates, who saw him as a threat to the oligarchic republic.

In 49 BC, tensions between Caesar and the Senate came to a head. Caesar had amassed great military power as general of the legions in Gaul, and many senators, led by Pompey, began to view him as a potential dictator. The Senate, dominated by the optimates, demanded that Caesar disband his army and return to Rome as a private citizen. Caesar, aware that he would be prosecuted by his enemies if he did so, decided to cross the Rubicon with his troops, an act that sparked a civil war against Pompey and his allies.

Caesar emerged victorious from the civil war, and in the years that followed he consolidated his power as perpetual dictator, a position that effectively made him the supreme leader of Rome. Although he attempted to implement important reforms, such as expanding the Senate and redistributing land, many saw this as the end of the republic. Despite his promises to restore republican order, the near-total control he exercised over the government and the military created fear in the political class.

The assassination of Julius Caesar was the result of a conspiracy orchestrated by a group of senators who believed that his power was a mortal threat to the republic. These men, who saw themselves as defenders of ancient republican traditions, feared that Caesar was preparing the ground for himself to become king, a hated position in Roman history since the expulsion of the Etruscan monarchs in the 6th century BC.

One of the key conspirators was Marcus Junius Brutus, who, despite being close to Caesar and linked to him by family ties, was a fervent republican. Others such as Gaius Cassius Longinus also joined the conspiracy, convinced that the only way to save the republic was to remove Caesar.

As Caesar's power grew, so did the paranoia among the senators. In February 44 BC, the Senate granted him the title of "perpetual dictator," which many interpreted as a sign that Caesar no longer intended to return power to the Senate or restore the republican balance. The situation was made worse when Caesar did not reject the symbols of monarchy. According to Plutarch, on one occasion during Lupercalia, a Roman festival, Mark Antony offered a crown to Caesar, who symbolically rejected it, but the scene left doubts about his true intentions.

On March 15, 44 BC, on the Ides of March, the conspirators executed their plan. They knew that Caesar would come to the Senate, where they were waiting for him with weapons hidden under their togas. As Caesar sat in Pompey's Curia, he was surrounded by the conspirators, who, one by one, stabbed him. Caesar is said to have been stabbed 23 times in total, although only one was fatal.

The death of Julius Caesar was a brutal and chaotic event. According to sources, Caesar attempted to defend himself at first, but upon recognizing Brutus among the attackers, he is said to have exclaimed the famous phrase: "You too, Brutus?" (although some historians doubt the authenticity of these words).

The conspirators, known as the Liberators, believed that by assassinating Caesar, they would restore the republic. However, their plan failed. Instead of saving Rome, Caesar's assassination unleashed a new wave of civil wars that eventually led to the rise of his adopted son, Octavian (Augustus), and the establishment of the Roman Empire.

The Roman people, far from celebrating Caesar's death, were enraged. Caesar was extremely popular among the lower classes and war veterans, who considered him their defender. In the days following his assassination, his funeral became a mass protest, and the conspirators were forced to flee Rome.

Ultimately, Caesar's death did not prevent the end of the republic; on the contrary, it accelerated the transition to a new political system. The story of his assassination, loaded with symbolism, remains a reminder of how power, ambition, and betrayal can change the course of history.

2. The Assassination of Abraham Lincoln: A Crime That Marked American History

On April 14, 1865, five days after the end of the American Civil War, President Abraham Lincoln was assassinated by John Wilkes Booth while attending a play at Ford's Theatre in Washington, D.C. This assassination, which had a profound impact on the history of the United States, was not only the tragic end to the life of one of the country's most iconic presidents but also a reflection of the deep divisions that continued to affect the nation after the bloodiest conflict in its history.

To understand the assassination of Abraham Lincoln, it is essential to understand the political and social situation that the United States was going through in the mid-19th century. The American Civil War (1861-1865) was a conflict between the North (the Union) and the South (the Confederate States), which arose primarily from tensions over slavery and states' rights.

Abraham Lincoln was elected president in 1860 as the candidate of the Republican Party, a political platform opposed to the expansion of slavery into the new territories of the United States. His election was seen as an existential threat to the southern states, whose economy and society depended on slave labor. Shortly after his election, seven southern states seceded from the Union and formed the Confederate States of America, which were later joined by four other states.

The war that followed was brutal, leaving more than 600,000 dead, and became a fight not only for the preservation of the Union but also for the abolition of slavery. On January 1, 1863, Lincoln issued the Emancipation Proclamation, a document declaring all slaves in the rebellious states free. This measure, while not immediately eliminating slavery nationwide, symbolized the Union government's commitment to ending this institution.

As the war progressed, Union victories, such as the Battle of Gettysburg in 1863 and the surrender of Confederate forces in April 1865, ensured victory for the North. However, even though the war was coming to an end, tensions surrounding the reconstruction of the country and the integration of former slaves into

American society continued to create a volatile environment.

Lincoln's assassination was carried out by John Wilkes Booth, a well-known actor and ardent sympathizer of the Confederate cause. Booth, born into a prominent acting family, was a staunch supporter of slavery and a vehement critic of Lincoln. He viewed the president as a tyrant who had destroyed the South, and his hatred of Lincoln grew as the war progressed.

Although Booth enjoyed a successful career in the theater, his ideology led him to engage in more radical activities. Initially, he did not plan to assassinate Lincoln, but rather to kidnap him and use him as a bargaining chip to force the Union to release Confederate prisoners. However, as the war ended and Confederate forces were in retreat, Booth decided to take more drastic action: assassinate the president, in the hopes of destabilizing the government and reinvigorating the Confederate cause.

Booth did not act alone; he was part of a larger conspiracy that included several accomplices, who also planned to assassinate other Union government leaders, including Vice President Andrew Johnson and Secretary of State William Seward. Booth believed that by eliminating these key leaders, he would throw the government into chaos, allowing Confederate sympathizers to regroup and regain control.

On April 14, 1865, Booth learned that Lincoln would be attending a performance of the play "Our American Cousin" at Ford's Theatre that evening. Taking advantage of his knowledge of the venue and his access as an actor, Booth planned to enter the presidential box during the play and assassinate Lincoln. That same night, other members of the conspiracy attempted to kill William Seward at his home, though they failed, and another accomplice was to assassinate the vice president but chickened out at the last moment.

Booth waited until the play's moment was generating laughter and sneaked into the box where Lincoln, his wife Mary Todd Lincoln, Major Henry Rathbone, and his fiancée were all sitting. At approximately 10:15 p.m., Booth shot Lincoln in the head at point-blank range with a derringer pistol. After firing, Booth leaped from the box onto the stage and reportedly shouted "Sic semper tyrannis!" (Thus always to tyrants, a phrase attributed to Brutus at the assassination of Julius Caesar.)

Seriously wounded, Lincoln was rushed to a nearby house, where he lay in a coma for several hours before dying at 7:22 a.m. on April 15, 1865.

Lincoln's assassination shocked the nation. Joy at victory over the Confederacy and the end of the war quickly turned to mourning. Lincoln had become an almost sacred figure to many Americans, especially in the North, for his leadership during the war and his commitment to the abolition of slavery.

Following the assassination, Booth fled Washington with the help of accomplices and remained on the run for 12 days, until he was found on a farm in Virginia, where he was shot dead by Union soldiers. His accomplices were captured and put on trial; four of them were executed for their role in the plot.

Lincoln's death had a profound impact on the course of Reconstruction. Lincoln's successor, Vice President Andrew Johnson, assumed the presidency at a critical moment in American history. Although Johnson attempted to follow Lincoln's policies of reconciliation with the South, his more lenient stances toward former Confederate leaders and his resistance to the full integration of African Americans into political life led to sharp clashes with the Congress, controlled by the Radical Republicans.

Lincoln's assassination removed a moderate leader who would likely have been able to more effectively manage the tensions of the Reconstruction period. Under Johnson's leadership, Reconstruction became a much more divisive process, leading to years of political and social conflict in the South, as well as the creation of laws that attempted to reverse some of the gains made during the war.

Lincoln became a martyr for the cause of freedom and unity, and his legacy as the president who preserved the Union and abolished slavery remains one of the most powerful in American history.

3. The Assassination of James A. Garfield: A Political Crime at the Height of Corruption and Nepotism

President James A. Garfield was assassinated in Washington D.C. on July 2, 1881, by Charles J. Guiteau, a frustrated seeker of government office. Although Garfield survived the initial shot, his death on September 19, 1881, after 79 days of suffering, was largely due to a lack of adequate medical care. Garfield's assassination shook the nation and highlighted the political tensions surrounding the system of political patronage and corruption that permeated the United States government in the late 19th century.

To understand the causes that led to Garfield's assassination, it is crucial to understand the political environment that prevailed in the United States in the 1880s. At that time, the political patronage system (also known as the "spoils system") was deeply rooted in the government. This system allowed elected officials, especially the president, to appoint their supporters and political allies to public office. These appointments were often based on political loyalties rather than merit or qualifications, which fostered corruption and nepotism.

After the American Civil War, corruption was widespread in various government agencies, and many politicians used their positions to reward their allies and entrench their power. While this system benefited political leaders, it also caused growing unrest in sectors of the country that advocated for a reform of the civil service based on merit and competence. In the late 1870s, this issue became one of the most polarizing issues in American politics.

James A. Garfield was elected president in 1880 as the Republican Party candidate, but his election was not an easy road. The Republican Party was divided into two main factions: the "stalwarts," led by Roscoe Conkling, who defended the patronage system and opposed civil service reform; and the "half-breeds," who advocated political reform and the elimination of corruption in government. Garfield belonged to the "half-breeds," and his election was seen as a threat by the stalwarts, who feared losing their power and influence in government.

After his election, Garfield attempted to balance both factions within his administration but quickly faced internal tensions. One of the critical points of conflict was his confrontation with Roscoe Conkling over the appointment of key officials, such as the post of collector of customs in New York, an extremely influential and coveted position at that time.

This internal political conflict and patronage demand not only exacerbated divisions in the Republican Party but also fueled the frustrations of those who hoped to obtain government office based on political promises. Among these was Charles J. Guiteau, who mistakenly believed that he had played a major role in Garfield's election and expected a reward in the form of a diplomatic post.

Charles J. Guiteau was a failed lawyer and an opportunist with delusions of grandeur. He had written a pamphlet in support of Garfield's candidacy and, in the aftermath, began applying for a government post, believing that his support had been crucial to Garfield's victory. Guiteau was convinced that he deserved a diplomatic post, specifically the post of consul in Paris, despite having no experience or credentials to hold such a position.

For months, Guiteau harassed members of the government with letters and requests for Garfield to grant him the post he craved, but his requests were ignored. As time passed and his hopes of gaining office faded, Guiteau developed a deep resentment toward the president. Through a series of delusions, he came to believe that he was destined to kill Garfield to "save the nation" and unite the Republican Party under the leadership of the stalwarts.

In Guiteau's mind, his act would be seen as a patriotic sacrifice, and he expected to be rewarded or at least glorified for his actions. This irrational and megalomaniacal reasoning led him to decide to assassinate Garfield.

On July 2, 1881, Charles Guiteau followed President James A. Garfield to the Baltimore and Potomac Railroad Station in Washington D.C. Garfield was on his way to an official visit, accompanied by his Secretary of State, James G. Blaine. Without a security escort (a common occurrence at the time), Garfield was walking nonchalantly when Guiteau, armed with a revolver, approached and shot him in the back twice.

One of the shots hit Garfield in the arm, while the other lodged in his back, near his spine. Although Garfield did not die instantly, his injuries were severe, and doctors struggled for weeks to save his life. Unfortunately, inadequate medical techniques and a lack of understanding of antisepsis at the time made matters worse. Doctors used unsterilized instruments and repeatedly probed the wounds in search of the bullet, leading to fatal infections.

Despite his resilience, Garfield succumbed to the infections and died on September 19, 1881, 79 days after being wounded.

Following the attack, Guiteau was immediately arrested and tried for murder. During his trial, Guiteau was erratic, interrupting the court and proclaiming himself to be a divine instrument. Although he attempted to argue that he was not responsible for his actions because he believed in a "divine mandate," the court found him guilty. He was sentenced to death and executed by hanging on June 30, 1882.

Garfield's murder, although committed by a mentally unstable man, highlighted the toxicity of the patronage system that fostered unreasonable expectations among political supporters. Guiteau was not the only petitioner frustrated by the system, but his case was notable for the violence to which his frustration led.

Garfield's assassination had a profound impact on American politics, especially patronage reform. His successor, Vice President Chester A. Arthur, a former stalwart, was initially seen as a defender of the patronage system, but Garfield's murder prompted him to change his stance.

In 1883, under President Arthur, the Pendleton Civil Service Reform Act was passed, establishing a merit-based system for hiring civil servants. The act created the Civil Service Commission, which oversaw competitive examinations to select government employees, largely ending the political reward system that had dominated for decades.

Civil service reform was one of the major consequences of Garfield's assassination and a crucial step in the fight against corruption and nepotism in the United States government. In addition, his death led to greater recognition of the need to improve the security of public officials, although this did not fully materialize until the 20th century.

The assassination of James A. Garfield was a tragic example of how the corrupt political system of patronage and the distorted expectations of applicants for government office could lead to violence. Although Garfield was the victim of a mentally unstable man, his death had a lasting impact on American politics, contributing to the implementation of key civil service reforms.

4. The assassination of Queen Min of Korea (1895): A political crime and the conflict of powers in Asia

The assassination of Queen Min, the last queen of the Joseon dynasty in Korea, on October 8, 1895, was a crucial event that marked a turning point in Korean history. The assassination was carried out by

Japanese agents in collaboration with pro-Japanese Korean factions, in a context of intense political and social tensions in the country. The rise of Japanese imperialism and Korea's struggle to maintain its sovereignty, amid the influence of foreign powers such as Japan, China, and Russia, were key factors in this assassination.

In the second half of the 19th century, Korea, under the Joseon dynasty, was in a serious political and social crisis. As foreign powers competed for influence in Asia, Korea found itself at the center of this power struggle. Japan, China, and Russia sought to expand their influence on the Korean peninsula, and the Korean government, weakened by internal corruption and lack of reform, was increasingly vulnerable to foreign interference.

For centuries, Korea had maintained a tribute relationship with China under the Qing dynasty, but this influence was threatened by the expansion of Japanese imperial power following the Meiji Restoration in 1868. Japan, which had begun an accelerated process of modernization and military expansion, viewed Korea as a crucial territory for its strategy of imperial growth in Asia. This clash of influences and ambitions between Japan and China had a profound impact on Korean politics.

Queen Min, whose posthumous name is Empress Myeongseong, became the wife of King Gojong of Korea in 1866. From her position as queen consort, Min became deeply involved in the country's political affairs, being a key figure in resisting the growing influence of Japan. She was known for her political intelligence and her staunch defense of Korean interests, seeking to counter Japanese expansionism through alliances with other foreign powers, especially Russia.

As Japan consolidated its influence on the Korean Peninsula, Queen Min actively worked to strengthen Korea's ties with China and Russia, seeing these alliances to slow Japanese advance. Her political stance made her a target for pro-Japanese factions in Korea, as well as the interests of the Japanese government itself, which saw her as an obstacle to its control over the region.

In 1894, the First Sino-Japanese War (1894–1895) broke out because of competition between China and Japan for influence in Korea. China's defeat in the war significantly weakened its position in Asia and the Treaty of Shimonoseki of 1895 consolidated Japan as the dominant power in Korea. However, Queen Min continued to resist growing Japanese influence, intensifying her efforts to forge alliances with Russia.

In the face of Queen Min's increasing resistance, the Japanese government decided to take drastic measures. In October 1895, a group of Japanese agents, led by Colonel Miura Gorō, together with pro-Japanese Korean factions, planned the assassination of the queen. The intention behind the attempt was to eliminate the leading figure of resistance to Japanese rule and consolidate Japan's control over Korean politics.

In the early morning of October 8, 1895, assassins, disguised as Korean soldiers, stormed Gyeongbokgung

Palace in Seoul. They brutally attacked Queen Min, murdering her in her chambers. The details of the assassination are chilling; after killing her, her body was burned to erase any evidence of the crime. The assassination was executed in such a violent manner that it shocked not only Korea but also the international community, due to the brutality of the attack and Japan's direct involvement.

The assassination of Queen Min had profound repercussions on Korean politics and international relations in the region. Her death removed the main barrier to Japanese interests in Korea, allowing Japan to further consolidate its influence over the country. Following the assassination, Japan imposed greater control over the Korean administration, and King Gojong, fearing for his life, sought refuge in the Russian embassy in 1896, marking a time of diplomatic tension between Russia and Japan.

Despite Gojong's attempts to resist Japanese influence, the assassination of Queen Min severely weakened Korea's position. With the queen out of the political arena, Japan was able to implement a series of reforms and consolidate its power on the peninsula. This process culminated in Japan's annexation of Korea in 1910, an event that was preceded by growing Japanese influence in the region following Russia's defeat in the Russo-Japanese War (1904-1905).

Queen Min's assassination was not only a turning point in Korean history but also left a legacy in the development of Korean nationalism. Despite Japanese efforts to erase her memory, Queen Min became a symbol of Korean resistance against foreign imperialism. Her bravery and staunch opposition to foreign occupation resonated deeply with Koreans, fueling the independence movement that would emerge in the decades that followed.

Queen Min's legacy was vindicated during the 20th century, when Korea finally achieved independence from Japan in 1945, following World War II. Her memory continues to be honored as that of a courageous leader who fought to the very end for Korea's sovereignty and dignity in the face of foreign threats.

5. The assassination of William McKinley: An anarchist crime in the era of American Imperialism

The assassination of President William McKinley on September 6, 1901, during a visit to the Pan-American Exposition in Buffalo, New York, was an event that shocked the United States. The president was shot at point-blank range by Leon Czolgosz, an anarchist of Polish origin, and died eight days later, on September 14. This assassination was not only an act of violence against the president but a manifestation of the political and social tensions that were emerging in the United States and around the world in the transition to the twentieth century.

McKinley's assassination was the result of a convergence of factors: the rise of international anarchism, the dissatisfaction of impoverished sectors with the political and economic system, and the profound transformations that the United States was experiencing as a new imperialist power.

In the late 19th and early 20th centuries, the United States was in the process of expansion and consolidation as a world power. The Spanish-American War of 1898 marked the beginning of direct US intervention in global affairs, after which the country acquired important territories, such as Puerto Rico, Guam, and the Philippines, and consolidated its influence in Cuba. This territorial and military expansion reflected the imperialist ambitions of a rising nation seeking to compete with European colonial powers.

However, this expansion also generated internal divisions in American society. While many celebrated the rise of the United States as a great power, others criticized the moral and political implications of imperialism. Anti-imperialist movements gained strength, arguing that the acquisition of colonies contradicted the democratic principles on which the country was founded.

In addition, the American economy was undergoing a radical transformation, with the growth of industrial capitalism. Although this brought prosperity to some, it also exacerbated social and economic disparities. Workers suffered from poor working conditions, long hours, and low wages, which contributed to the growth of trade union movements and the emergence of more radical political currents, such as socialism and anarchism.

In this context, anarchism emerged as a radical ideology that rejected the state, authority, and capitalism, proposing a society without hierarchies. In Europe and the United States, anarchism gained followers among workers and the marginalized who saw the political and economic system as a source of oppression. Anarchists advocated direct action as a form of struggle, and some saw political assassinations (known as "propaganda by the deed") as a legitimate means of dismantling power and promoting revolution.

The 1890s saw a series of attacks and assassinations in Europe and North America. In 1894, French President Sadi Carnot was assassinated by an anarchist. In 1897, Empress Elisabeth of Austria, known as Sissi, was also the victim of an anarchist attack. This climate of global political violence coincided with the rise of labor and radical movements in the United States, where workers faced exploitation and repression.

Within this context, some anarchists in the United States, such as Leon Czolgosz, took extreme positions against the government and the economic system. Although the anarchist movement in general did not approve of the attacks, some isolated individuals acted on their own, as Czolgosz would do in his attack on William McKinley.

Leon Czolgosz was born to a family of Polish immigrants and grew up in poverty in the state of Michigan. He worked in factories from an early age but lost his job during the economic recession of 1893, a crisis that left millions of Americans in misery.

Disillusioned with the capitalist system and the society of his time, Czolgosz became politically radicalized.

In search of answers, Czolgosz began to become interested in anarchist ideas. He attended lectures by prominent anarchist leaders, such as Emma Goldman, who advocated a society free of state and economic oppression. Although he did not formally join any anarchist group, Czolgosz adopted the belief that governments were responsible for the exploitation and suffering of workers. Determined to do something to change this situation, Czolgosz became convinced that he should assassinate the president as a symbolic act to strike a blow against the oppressive power.

Czolgosz, inspired by the recent assassination of King Umberto I of Italy in 1900 by another anarchist, planned his attack on McKinley. He believed that by eliminating the president, he would spark a revolutionary movement and that his act would be seen as a sacrifice for the cause of the oppressed.

On September 6, 1901, William McKinley was participating in the Pan-American Exposition in Buffalo, New York, an international event designed to showcase the technological advances and economic progress of the American nations. McKinley, who had been re-elected to a second term, was popular with much of the public and represented a vision of a prosperous and expanding America.

During a public reception at the Temple of Music on the exposition grounds, Czolgosz approached the president as he stood in a line of people waiting to greet him. He had a gun concealed under a handkerchief in his hand. When McKinley extended his hand to shake his, Czolgosz fired two shots at point-blank range. One bullet bounced off the button of McKinley's jacket, but the other hit his abdomen.

McKinley was quickly treated by doctor's present at the exposition, but surgical techniques at the time were not advanced, and the wound became infected. Despite efforts to save his life, McKinley died on September 14, 1901.

The assassination of William McKinley had profound repercussions on American politics. His death brought to power Vice President Theodore Roosevelt, a young and energetic politician who would assume the presidency at the age of 42, becoming the youngest president in the history of the United States. Roosevelt would implement a series of progressive reforms, aimed at limiting the power of large monopolies and improving labor conditions, in response to the social and political tensions that had led to McKinley's assassination.

In addition, the assassination of McKinley generated increasing paranoia and repression towards anarchists and other radical movements in the United States. Shortly after the assassination, laws were passed that facilitated the deportation of foreigners linked to anarchist ideologies, and the federal government intensified its efforts to repress the movement. The Czolgosz case also exposed the vulnerability of American presidents, which eventually led to greater protection and security for presidents.

6. The Assassination of Francisco I. Madero: The End of the Democratic Revolution and the Rise of Military Violence

The assassination of Francisco I. Madero, President of Mexico, on February 22, 1913, marked a tragic turning point in the country's political history. Madero, an idealistic leader who had led the fight against the dictatorial regime of Porfirio Díaz and ushered in the start of the Mexican Revolution in 1910, was betrayed by his army in what became known as the Tragic Ten Days, a bloody coup d'état orchestrated by General Victoriano Huerta.

The context surrounding Madero's assassination reflects the social, political, and military tensions that defined the early years of the Mexican Revolution and shows how the democratic and social justice ideals that Madero championed were crushed by military power and the interests of conservative elites.

At the beginning of the 20th century, Mexico was living under the dictatorship of Porfirio Díaz, who had ruled the country almost uninterruptedly since 1876. Díaz's regime, known as the Porfiriato, was characterized by strong authoritarian control, support for the interests of the landed and business elites, and a policy of openness to foreign capital that favored economic growth, but at the cost of great social inequalities. Most of the rural population lived in extreme poverty, while the elite accumulated wealth and power.

In 1908, Díaz made the famous declaration that Mexico was ready for democracy and that he would not seek reelection in the next elections. This encouraged

Francisco I. Madero, a northern landowner with democratic ideals and a reformist vision, ran as a candidate in the 1910 presidential elections. Madero advocated democracy, effective suffrage, and limiting the power of the elites. His book "The Presidential Succession in 1910" called for a peaceful transition of power and was the catalyst for the creation of a broad movement seeking Díaz's downfall.

However, Díaz was unwilling to give up power, so he manipulated the 1910 elections, fraudulently declaring himself the winner. Faced with this situation, Madero fled to the United States and from there launched the Plan of San Luis, in which he called on the Mexican people to rise in arms against the Díaz regime. On November 20, 1910, the Mexican Revolution began, with Madero as its symbolic leader.

In 1911, after several months of revolutionary struggle and with the Díaz regime weakened, the dictator finally resigned and went into exile in France. Madero was elected president in a democratic election, taking office in November 1911. However, his government soon faced multiple challenges.

Madero believed strongly in the need for national reconciliation and the construction of a liberal democracy, but his moderate approach was criticized by both conservative sectors and radical revolutionaries. Although he had come to power thanks to a revolution, Madero was reluctant to implement deep reforms that would satisfy peasants and workers, who demanded a fair distribution of land and labor improvements. At the same time, he attempted to govern within the margins of Porfirian institutions, which alienated the more radical sectors of his movement.

Among Madero's critics was the revolutionary leader Emiliano Zapata, who advocated the immediate return of land to peasants under the Plan of Ayala, and who considered Madero to have betrayed the ideals of the revolution. At the same time, Pascual Orozco, another revolutionary leader, also rebelled against Madero, frustrated by the lack of significant changes in the country's economic and political structure.

As his government faced economic difficulties, internal rebellions, and growing opposition from conservatives and Porfirian elites who wished to restore the old order, Madero turned to the military to maintain control. However, this decision would prove fatal. Within the army there were still many loyalists to the old regime, and among them was General Victoriano Huerta, an experienced military man who had been appointed by Madero to put down the rebellions.

Between February 9 and 19, 1913, a violent military uprising took place in Mexico City known as the Tragic Ten Days. The coup was led by General Félix Díaz, nephew of Porfirio Díaz, and Bernardo Reyes, a Porfirista general. Although Madero initially trusted Huerta to defend his government, the general ended up betraying him. With the tacit support of the United States ambassador, Henry Lane Wilson, Huerta secretly negotiated with the coup plotters.

On February 18, 1913, Huerta arrested Madero and Vice President José María Pino Suárez in a coup d'état that marked the end of his brief democratic government. Despite Huerta's promises to spare Madero's life, on February 22, 1913, Madero and Pino Suárez were murdered in cold blood while being transferred to Lecumberri prison. The official version claimed that they had been shot down in an escape attempt, but it was widely known that Huerta had ordered their execution.

Madero's assassination was also influenced by the international context, by US interests in Mexico. Under President William Taft, the US government had watched with concern the reforms and political instability in Mexico, a key country for its economic and strategic interests, especially due to its oil wealth.

The US ambassador to Mexico, Henry Lane Wilson, played a key role in the coup against Madero. Wilson, a pro-business diplomat, saw Madero as a threat to US interests and actively supported Huerta in his plans for his overthrow. His complicity in the coup and the assassination of Madero was a clear example of US intervention in Mexico's internal politics, which increased distrust towards the northern country in the following years.

Madero's assassination and Huerta's rise to power marked the end of the first phase of the Mexican Revolution and the beginning of a new stage of struggle. Huerta's regime was quickly condemned by the revolutionaries who had fought against Díaz, and leaders such as Venustiano Carranza, Pancho Villa, and Emiliano Zapata took up arms against Huerta's dictatorship under the slogan of restoring legality and social justice.

Huerta's dictatorship was brutal and repressive, but it faced widespread resistance. In 1914, after a series of military defeats and under pressure from the United States, Huerta was forced to resign, opening the way for a new phase of the Mexican Revolution. However, Madero's assassination had left a deep mark on the revolutionary movement. Its democratic and reconciliation ideals were overshadowed by the violence, chaos, and power struggle that would dominate Mexico in the years that followed.

Today, Madero is remembered as the "Apostle of Democracy," a martyr whose dream of a free and democratic Mexico was snatched away prematurely, but whose vision remains an inspiration in the fight for justice and equality in the country.

7. The Assassination of Tsar Nicholas II and his Family: The End of the Romanov Dynasty and the Russian Revolution

The assassination of Tsar Nicholas II of Russia and his family in the early morning of July 17, 1918, in Yekaterinburg marked the tragic end of a dynasty that had ruled Russia for more than 300 years. This assassination was not only a brutal act of political violence but also the climax of social and political tensions that had rocked the Russian Empire for decades, culminating in the Russian Revolution of 1917 and the establishment of Bolshevik rule.

At the beginning of the 20th century, Russia was a vast multi-ethnic empire ruled by the tsars of the Romanov dynasty. However, the country was plagued by social and political tensions. Despite being one of the largest powers in Europe, Russia was a backward country compared to other industrialized nations. Most of its population lived in conditions of extreme poverty, working in agriculture, and there was deep inequality between the landed elite and the vast peasant majority.

Tsar Nicholas II, who ascended the throne in 1894, was an autocrat convinced that absolute power should reside in the figure of the monarch. However, his leadership was widely perceived as ineffective and disconnected from the needs of the people. His rigidity and unwillingness to reform the country's political and economic system aggravated the crisis. Despite demands for reform, Nicholas II maintained a firm grip on the government, suppressing revolts with violence.

The situation was aggravated by the Revolution of 1905, sparked by widespread discontent following Russia's defeat in the war with Japan (1904-1905) and the harsh living conditions of workers and peasants. Although the Tsar attempted to calm tensions by creating the Duma (Russian parliament), reforms were limited, and dissatisfaction persisted.

When World War I broke out in 1914, Russia joined the Allied coalition against the Central Powers. However, Russian participation in the war proved disastrous. Poorly equipped and led, the Russian army suffered heavy defeats at the hands of the Germans. As the war progressed, casualties mounted, and hunger and misery spread throughout the country. The population, exhausted by deprivation and lack of food, blamed the Tsarist government for the situation.

The war exacerbated already existing social tensions. Tsar Nicholas II made the fatal mistake of personally assuming command of the army in 1915, leaving the administration of the government in the hands of his wife, Tsarina Alexandra, who was influenced by the mystic Rasputin, which generated even more distrust and contempt among the nobility and the people. Rasputin, although detested by many members of the Russian elite, had enormous influence over the Tsarina due to his ability to alleviate the hemophilia of Tsarevich Alexei, the heir to the throne. His influence and scandals contributed to undermining the legitimacy of the government.

By early 1917, the situation in Russia had become untenable. The combination of military defeats, famine, and discontent led to a massive uprising known as the February Revolution of 1917. Under overwhelming pressure, Tsar Nicholas II abdicated on March 15, 1917, ending more than three centuries of Romanov rule.

Following the abdication, a Provisional Government, led by moderate figures such as Alexander Kerensky, attempted to maintain control of the country but was unable to cope with the growing chaos. The war continued, social divisions deepened, and radical factions, such as the Bolsheviks led by Vladimir Lenin, gained popularity with their promise of "peace, bread and land."

In October 1917, the Bolsheviks seized power in a coup known as the October Revolution. Lenin and his followers established a communist government based on Marxist ideology, which aimed to create a socialist state where power was in the hands of workers and peasants.

Meanwhile, the Romanov family was under house arrest. Initially, they were held in the palace at Tsarskoye Selo and then moved to Tobolsk in Siberia as the Russian civil war between the Bolsheviks and counter-revolutionary forces (the "Whites") escalated. However, the threat of the Whites freeing the family increased as anti-communist troops advanced into the territories where the Romanovs were being held captive.

In April 1918, the family was moved to Yekaterinburg in the Ural Mountains, where they were confined in the Ipatiev House. The Bolsheviks saw Nicholas II as a symbolic threat to the revolution, as his figure could be used by the regime's enemies to justify a monarchical restoration. As the civil war continued, the family's situation became increasingly precarious.

In the early hours of July 17, 1918, the Romanov family—Tsar Nicholas II, his wife Alexandra, their daughters Olga, Tatiana, Maria, and Anastasia, and their son Alexei—was brutally murdered by a group of Bolshevik soldiers under the orders of the Ural Council, a local faction of the Soviet government. Some servants who were with them also died.

The murder was carried out summarily in the basement of the Ipatiev House. According to historical accounts, the family was awakened in the middle of the night and ordered to dress, under the pretext of being moved to a safer location. Once in the basement, they were told to wait until they were escorted to another location. Without warning, soldiers, led by Yakov Yurovsky, entered the room and read out an order for their execution. Nicholas barely had time to react before he was shot at point-blank range.

The rest of the family and their servants were also executed. Because some members of the family wore jewelry sewn into their clothes as a protective measure, the bullets did not kill them immediately, resulting in a violent and chaotic execution. After the murder, the bodies were taken to a nearby forest, where they were buried and partially dissolved in acid to prevent their identification.

The murder of the Romanovs was a brutal event, but also a symbolic act. By executing the last tsar and his family, the Bolsheviks closed a chapter in Russian history, eliminating any possibility of monarchical restoration and consolidating their control over the country. The Russian Civil War continued until 1923, but the communist regime emerged victorious, establishing the Soviet Union under the leadership of Lenin and, later, Stalin.

For many Russians and international observers, the murder of the Romanovs was a sign of the Bolsheviks' ruthlessness and the magnitude of change taking place in Russia. The elimination of the imperial family represented not only the end of autocracy but also the destruction of old Russia and the creation of a new society based on the revolutionary principles of socialism.

For decades, the fate of the Romanovs was shrouded in mystery, and many legends arose about possible survivors, particularly about Grand Duchess Anastasia. However, in 1991, the family remains were exhumed and DNA analysis confirmed the Romanovs' identity. In 2000, the Russian Orthodox Church canonized Nicholas II, his wife, and their children as martyrs.

The assassination of Nicholas II and his family is remembered as a pivotal moment in Russian history. For some, it represents the extreme violence of the Russian Revolution; for others, it symbolizes the end of centuries of monarchical oppression. In any case, the assassination of the Romanovs remains one of the most controversial and poignant episodes in modern history.

8. The assassination of Archduke Franz Ferdinand of Austria: The catalyst for World War I

The assassination of Archduke Franz Ferdinand of Austria on June 28, 1914, in Sarajevo marked a crucial turning point in modern history, triggering World War I and altering the political map of Europe forever. Franz Ferdinand, heir to the throne of the Austro-Hungarian Empire, was assassinated along with his wife, Duchess Sophie, against a backdrop of nationalist tensions, imperial rivalries, and complex alliances that defined European politics at the time.

At the beginning of the 20th century, the Austro-Hungarian Empire faced increasing internal pressure due to its diverse nationalities. The empire was composed of multiple ethnic groups, including Austrians, Hungarians, Czechs, Slovaks, Poles, Serbs, and Croats, among others. The mix of cultures and languages, while rich, generated significant tensions, especially among Slavic nations that aspired to independence or unification with other ethnic groups, such as the Serbs.

Slavic nationalism had intensified in recent decades, partly in response to cultural and political oppression by the Austro-Hungarian government. In this context, the figure of Serbia emerged as a symbol of resistance for the southern Slavs, who sought to unite under a single banner. The creation of the Kingdom of Serbs, Croats, and Slovenes (later Yugoslavia) was a desired goal for many nationalists in the region.

The climate of political unrest led to the rise of radical groups advocating the unification of Slavic peoples. One of these groups was the Black Hand, a secret Serbian nationalist organization that sought to liberate the Slavs from Austro-Hungarian rule through acts of violence. The Black Hand enjoyed military and logistical support from some sections of the Serbian army and viewed Archduke Franz Ferdinand as a direct enemy due to his authoritarian stance and role in the administration of the empire.

The Archduke had expressed his intentions to implement reforms in the empire, including greater autonomy for Slavic peoples, but many nationalists felt that his government would continue to perpetuate oppression. Therefore, his visit to Sarajevo, scheduled for 28 June 1914, was perceived as a provocation and an opportunity to make a dramatic statement against the Austro-Hungarian regime.

On 28 June 1914, the Archduke and his wife arrived in Sarajevo for an official visit. The day began with several failed assassination attempts. The first attack was carried out by Nedeljko Cabrinovic, one of the Black Hand conspirators, who threw a grenade at the Archduke's car. However, the bomb misfired and exploded behind the car, injuring several of the passengers.

After the failed attack, Franz Ferdinand decided to visit the wounded in the hospital, but his route was altered due to the confusion caused by the attack. During the journey, the driver of the vehicle carrying the Archduke took a wrong turn and stopped right in front of a café where Gavrilo Princip, another member of the Black Hand, was present. In a twist of fate, Princip, who had been in the right place at the right time, approached the car and fired two bullets, hitting Franz Ferdinand and his wife. Both died shortly after.

The attack set off a series of chain reactions that led to the mobilization of military and political alliances in Europe. The Austro-Hungarian government, with the support of Germany, decided to act forcefully against Serbia, whom they accused of having instigated the attack. On July 23, 1914, Austria-Hungary issued an ultimatum to Serbia with extremely severe conditions, which were mostly, but not entirely, accepted. This provided the perfect excuse for the empire to declare war on Serbia on July 28.

The declaration of war triggered the activation of several military alliances in Europe. Russia, an ally of Serbia, began to mobilize its troops, leading Germany to declare war on Russia on August 1 and France on August 3. Thus, what began as a regional conflict quickly transformed into a world war, involving multiple nations and changing the balance of power in Europe.

The assassination of Franz Ferdinand is considered the triggering event for World War I, a conflict that would stretch into 1918 and cause the deaths of millions of people and the destruction of vast regions of Europe. The consequences of the war were profound, resulting in the collapse of empires, such as the Austro-Hungarian and Ottoman Empires, and the rise of new nation-states in Europe and the Middle East.

The 1919 Treaty of Versailles, which ended the war, set harsh conditions for Germany and its allies, sowing resentments that would lead to World War II in the following decades. The reconfiguration of the map of Europe and the establishment of new national borders, based on principles of self-determination, laid the groundwork for future conflicts in the 20th century.

9. The assassination attempt on Adolf Hitler: The conspiracy of the Wehrmacht officers and the context of the Third Reich

The assassination attempt on Adolf Hitler, carried out on July 20, 1944, known as Operation Valkyrie, is one of the most intriguing and dramatic episodes in the history of Nazi Germany. This assassination attempt, which was orchestrated by a group of Wehrmacht officers (the German army), occurred in the context of growing discontent with the Nazi regime, the devastation of World War II, and the longing for political change in Germany.

By mid-1944, Germany's situation in World War II had become critical. Following the defeat at the Battle of Stalingrad (1942-1943) and the Normandy landings in June 1944, the Third Reich faced a bleak military outlook. Allied forces were advancing from the west, while the Soviet army was pushing from the east. The morale of the German people and the army was in decline, and the country was mired in an economic and social crisis.

Hitler's regime, which had been built on the pillars of extreme nationalism, anti-Semitism, and militarism, was beginning to be questioned even within its ranks. As the war progressed, many Wehrmacht officers realized that the ideology of Nazism and Hitler's decisions were leading Germany to ruin. These officers, mostly conservative and patriotic, were aware that the only way to save what was left of Germany was to eliminate Hitler and negotiate peace with the Allies.

Among the plotters of the attack were prominent figures in the German army, such as Colonel Claus von Stauffenberg, who became the key figure in the execution of the plan. Stauffenberg, an officer with a strong sense of patriotism and disillusioned by the direction the Nazi regime had taken, was convinced that action against Hitler was necessary to prevent further disaster.

Operation Valkyrie was originally intended as a contingency plan to maintain control in Germany in the event of internal unrest following Hitler's death. However, the plotters decided to use this plan to assassinate the Führer.

On 20 July 1944, Stauffenberg, who had been assigned to Hitler's headquarters in Berlin, managed to smuggle a bomb into a meeting in the Wolfsschanze (Wolf's Lair) bunker in East Prussia, where Hitler was meeting with several senior army officers. The bomb was designed to detonate after a scheduled delay, allowing Stauffenberg to escape the premises.

The attack was carried out on the evening of 20 July. Stauffenberg placed the bomb in the conference room and then quickly left the premises. However, the plan was thwarted by a series of unforeseen circumstances. An assistant moved the suitcase containing the bomb away from Hitler, reducing its effectiveness. The explosion, although devastating, failed to kill the Führer, who suffered injuries but survived.

Although several high-ranking officers were killed in the explosion, Hitler was quickly taken to a safe place, where he received medical attention. Upon learning of

Hitler's survival, the conspirators realized that their plan had failed and consequently began to lose control of the situation.

Following the attack, the Nazi authorities unleashed a wave of repression. Hitler, furious at the betrayal, ordered an exhaustive search for the plotters. Many of them were arrested, tortured, and executed. Stauffenberg was captured and executed on the night of 21 July. In total, it is estimated that thousands of people were hunted down, arrested, and killed in the weeks following the attack, to crush any internal resistance to the regime.

The failure of the attack had devastating consequences for Germany. The repression intensified Hitler's control over the country and his determination to continue the war at all costs, even as defeat became increasingly clear. Nazi propaganda used the attack to demonize the plotters and consolidate popular support for the regime.

The July 1944 attack also falls within a broader context of social discontent in Germany. As the war progressed, the population faced food shortages, devastated cities, and constant suffering at the front. German citizens increasingly began to question the direction of the country and the ideology of Nazism.

Despite brutal repression, resistance to the Nazi regime was brewing in different sectors of society, from intellectuals to workers and youth. Although the Stauffenberg assassination failed to turn the tide of the war, it laid the groundwork for future expressions of resistance and questioning of the regime.

The assassination of Hitler failed to stop the Third Reich from marching towards its eventual collapse, but it did expose internal divisions within the regime and the growing desperation of those who opposed Nazi tyranny. The failure of the plot underlined the human cost of the regime's authoritarianism and brutality, which was carried out in the context of total war.

The fall of Hitler and the defeat of the Third Reich in 1945 brought with it the revelation of the horrors of the Holocaust and the atrocities committed in the name of Nazism. The story of the July 1944 conspiracy is remembered as an example of the internal struggle for morality and ethics in times of crisis.

10. The assassination attempt on King Abdullah I of Jordan: Political and social context amidst Arab Nationalism

The assassination attempt on King Abdullah I of Jordan on July 20, 1951, in the Old City of Jerusalem, was an event that marked a turning point in the history of Jordan and the Middle East. Abdullah, the first king of the Hashemite Kingdom of Jordan, was assassinated by an Arab nationalist in the context of political tensions, regional conflicts, and the growing fervor of Arab nationalism in the 1950s.

Abdullah I ascended the throne in 1946, following Jordan's independence from the British mandate. His reign was characterized by a pragmatic approach to regional politics and a constant search for stability in a tumultuous environment. From the beginning, Abdullah was faced with numerous challenges, including conflicts with Arab neighbors, popular resentment, and international pressure.

The creation of the state of Israel in 1948 and the ensuing Arab-Israeli War led to great instability in the region. Many Arabs, including Jordanians, viewed the creation of Israel as a betrayal of the Palestinian cause and the struggle for Arab self-determination. Abdullah I, who had supported the creation of a unified Arab state and an agreement with Israel, faced strong opposition from nationalist and pan-Arab quarters.

As Arab nationalism gained strength in the region, many Arabs began to view Abdullah as a leader who did not adequately represent their aspirations. His relationship with the British and his moderate approach to the Arab-Israeli conflict further fueled discontent. Arab nationalists desired a more aggressive stance and greater solidarity with the Palestinian cause, which led to tensions in Jordanian society.

Popular pressure intensified following the Arab defeat in the 1948 War and continued territorial losses in the region. Abdullah was accused of betraying Arab interests and being a collaborator with the West, leading to increased hostility towards his government.

On 20 July 1951, Abdullah I was assassinated by Izz al-Din al-Qassam, a Palestinian Arab nationalist. During a visit to Jerusalem to attend the inauguration of the Al-Aqsa Mosque, Abdullah was attacked while inside the mosque. The attacker, who had infiltrated the crowd, shot the king several times, mortally wounding him.

Al-Qassam's motivations were deeply rooted in Arab nationalism and resentment towards any leader who appeared to give in to Western demands or seek reconciliation with Israel. Al-Qassam, like many of his contemporaries, viewed the king as having betrayed the Palestinian cause and that his death would be an act of resistance against a regime considered illegitimate.

The assassination of Abdullah I had significant repercussions for Jordan and the balance of power in the region. His death left a power vacuum at a critical time, and his son, Prince Talal, assumed the throne, although his reign was brief and complicated. Political instability increased and the new king faced significant internal and external challenges.

In addition, the bombing deepened divisions between moderate and nationalist sectors of Jordanian society. Arab nationalists, who saw Abdullah's assassination as a heroic act, continued to push their agenda, while moderates and those who supported greater cooperation with the West felt increasingly threatened.

The bombing also occurred in a broader Cold War context. Competition between the Western powers and the Soviet Union for influence in the Middle East influenced politics in the region. The search for stability in Jordan was further complicated by Soviet support for nationalist and communist movements in the Arab world.

During the 1950s, the political climate in the Middle East became increasingly volatile. The growing influence of Arab nationalism, driven by leaders such as Gamal Abdel Nasser in Egypt, led to a call for Arab unity that challenged the authority of traditional monarchs such as Abdullah and his successor, Talal.

The assassination of King Abdullah I of Jordan not only marked the end of his reign but also symbolized simmering tensions in the Arab world and the impact of nationalism on regional politics. His assassination exacerbated instability in Jordan and highlighted the internal struggles facing the kingdom at a time of profound and rapid change in the Middle East.

Abdullah's legacy and the context of his assassination remain relevant today, reflecting the complexities of politics in the region and the challenges facing Arab leaders in their search for stability and legitimacy amidst an ever-evolving nationalism. The story of Abdullah and his tragic end underscores the fragility of authoritarian regimes in the context of increasing demand for participation and representation in Arab politics.

11. The assassination of King Faisal II of Iraq: The end of the Hashemite Monarchy in a context of revolution and social change

The assassination of King Faisal II of Iraq on 14 July 1958 marked the end of the Hashemite monarchy in Iraq and symbolized a decisive moment in Middle

Eastern history. The assassination, which was part of a revolutionary military coup, reflected the political and social tensions that had been building up in Iraq for decades, amid a climate of regional instability, Arab nationalism, and resentment against colonialism and Western influence.

Faisal II, the grandson of Faisal I, belonged to the Hashemite dynasty, which had been installed on the Iraqi throne in 1921 by the British after World War I. The Hashemite monarchy in Iraq had deep connections to the British Mandate, which led to internal tensions. Although Faisal II officially assumed the throne in 1953 upon coming of age, his rule was heavily influenced by his uncle, Prince Regent Abd al-Ilah, who had acted as a regent since Faisal's childhood.

During his reign, Faisal II attempted to govern in a complicated environment. Iraq was riven by ethnic, religious, and political tensions: the ruling elite was predominantly Sunni, while a large part of the population was Shia. In addition, there was a sizable Kurdish population in the north that also sought greater autonomy.

The monarchical government, perceived as pro-Western and dependent on British support, was viewed with increasing distrust by Arab nationalists, who criticized its close relationship with Western powers, especially at a time when Arab nationalism was on the rise under leaders such as Gamal Abdel Nasser in Egypt.

The 1950s witnessed growing discontent in the Arab world against traditional monarchies that were associated with former colonial powers. Arab nationalism, driven by Nasser and his vision of a greater Arab unity, was gaining adherents throughout the Middle East. In Iraq, pan-Arab aspirations and resentment against monarchical control and its ties to the West began to crystallize into opposition movements.

The 1955 Baghdad Treaty, a military alliance between Iraq, Turkey, Iran, Pakistan, and the United Kingdom, was one of the most controversial policies of Faisal II's monarchy. Signed under pressure from the British and the United States in the context of the Cold War, this treaty was perceived by many Iraqis as an instrument to maintain Western influence in the region and as a betrayal of Arab interests, especially in the fight against Israel.

In addition, internal social tensions in Iraq were increasing. The ruling class, which included the Sunni political and economic elite, was disconnected from the majority Shiite and Kurdish population, who felt marginalized and oppressed. Poverty, unemployment, and social inequality fueled popular resentment, while leftist and Arab nationalist movements were gaining strength.

The discontent culminated on July 14, 1958, when General Abd al-Karim Qasim, along with other Iraqi army officers, led a military coup that overthrew the monarchy. The coup was partly a response to the formation of the Arab Federation, a union between Iraq and Jordan established in February 1958, which was intended to counter the influence of Arab nationalism led by Nasser. This federation was seen by nationalist officers and much of the population as a continuation of British control in the region.

The army fed up with the status quo and animated by nationalist and pan-Arab ideas, saw an opportunity to change the course of Iraq. The coup began when troops heading to Jordan to reinforce the federation took control of Baghdad. Military forces stormed the royal palace and arrested King Faisal II, Prince Regent Abd al-Ilah, and other members of the royal family.

King Faisal II and his family were summarily executed in the courtyard of the royal palace. Although the king had initially been planned to be exiled, the situation spiraled out of control and the family was massacred without trial. Scenes of violence spread beyond the palace as supporters of the coup attacked other supporters of the Hashemite regime.

Images of Abd al-Ilah's mutilated corpse hanged and dragged through the streets of Baghdad, symbolised the brutal collapse of the monarchy. Faisal II, who had been a young 23-year-old king with few opportunities for independent politics, was killed along with almost the entire royal family, marking the end of an era.

Following Faisal II's assassination, Abd al-Karim Qasim assumed power, establishing the Republic of Iraq. The new regime was initially hailed by nationalist and socialist quarters, and Qasim attempted to implement social and economic reforms aimed at reducing poverty and improving the lot of the working classes.

However, the 1958 coup did not resolve the country's internal tensions. Although Qasim promised to rule in the name of the people, his regime soon faced challenges from other nationalist movements, including supporters of the Baath and communism. The Kurds also continued their struggles for autonomy, and Iraq's internal politics became increasingly fragmented.

The overthrow of the Hashemite monarchy in Iraq had a profound impact on the region. The fall of Faisal II was symbolic of the decline of traditional Middle Eastern monarchies and the rise of new political movements, based on Arab nationalism, socialism, and anti-colonialism. The 1958 coup also foreshadowed future revolts and conflicts in the Arab world, as countries sought to free themselves from Western influence and reorganize their systems of government.

The assassination of Faisal II not only meant the end of a dynasty but also the beginning of a new phase of political instability in Iraq, which would continue to struggle to find a balance between its various factions and national aspirations.

12. The assassination of John F. Kennedy: A crime shrouded in controversy

The assassination of John F. Kennedy on November 22, 1963, in Dallas, Texas, was one of the most shocking and tragic events in contemporary American history. The assassination not only ended the life of one of the most charismatic presidents in American history, but also shook confidence in institutions and deepened divisions in a society facing significant political, social, and economic challenges.

Kennedy's assassination occurred in a context marked by Cold War tensions, racial conflicts in the United States, and a series of social and political reforms that were not well received by all sectors of the country. To understand the impact of the JFK assassination, it is crucial to examine the political and social environment that preceded it.

John F. Kennedy assumed the presidency in January 1961, at a time when the world was gripped by Cold War tension between the United States and the Soviet Union. The rivalry between the two superpowers escalated in the aftermath of World War II, and both countries were engaged in ideological, economic, military, and space competition. During his time in the White House, Kennedy faced several significant challenges in this context, many of which increased tensions both abroad and at home.

One of the most critical moments of the Cold War during Kennedy's presidency was the Cuban Missile Crisis in October 1962. The discovery of Soviet nuclear missiles on Cuban soil, just 150 kilometers from the American coast, led to a confrontation between Washington and Moscow. Kennedy handled the crisis firmly, imposing a naval blockade on Cuba and secretly negotiating with Soviet leader Nikita Khrushchev to dismantle the missiles, avoiding a nuclear war. Although Kennedy emerged strengthened for his handling of the crisis, the incident increased paranoia and internal divisions in the United States, with many opposing his negotiating approach.

In addition, Kennedy also dealt with the Vietnam War, an intervention that was beginning to intensify during his term. Although Kennedy had initially sought a diplomatic solution, the American presence in Vietnam continued to grow. This conflict, which in the years following JFK's assassination would cause a strong division in American society, was already beginning to generate criticism towards his administration.

Domestically, Kennedy was a progressive president who promoted several economic and social reforms. However, one of the main challenges of his administration was the fight for civil rights. In the early 1960s, the United States was deeply divided on racial issues, with the South being a bastion of racial segregation policies. The civil rights movement, led by figures such as Martin Luther King Jr., was pushing to end legal discrimination against African Americans, especially in the southern states.

Kennedy was initially cautious in his support for the civil rights movement, fearing to alienate southern Democrats who were essential to his political coalition. However, faced with rising racial violence and growing demands for equality, in 1963 he decided to openly support a civil rights law, which would prohibit racial segregation in public spaces and guarantee equal access to education and employment. This decision put him at the center of controversy, especially in the southern states, where many considered his support for racial equality to be a threat to their way of life.

Racial tensions in the country contributed to social polarization and increased resentment towards Kennedy in certain sectors. In addition, unions and other progressive groups supported him in his economic reforms, while some conservative businessmen saw him as a threat to free market interests, intensifying political divisions.

Kennedy's assassination also occurred in a climate of increasing paranoia and conspiracy theories. The early 1960s were marked by fear of communism and the perception that the country was being infiltrated by internal enemies. During this period, J. Edgar Hoover, the director of the FBI, carried out extensive surveillance of political and social figures, many of whom were seen as communist sympathizers or dangerous to national security.

In addition, Kennedy had begun to distance himself from certain sectors of the military-industrial complex and the CIA, which advocated a more aggressive stance in the Cold War. Kennedy was reportedly unhappy with the CIA after the failed invasion attempt of Cuba at the Bay of Pigs in 1961, which led to internal friction within his administration.

These elements contributed to an environment in which suspicions and conspiracies abounded, which partly explains why Kennedy's assassination has been the subject of so many theories over the years. Indeed, to this day, many question whether the lone gunman, Lee Harvey Oswald, was solely responsible for the assassination or whether he was part of a larger conspiracy.

On November 22, 1963, Kennedy was on a political tour in Texas, a state where the Democratic Party was internally divided. While riding in a motorcade through the streets of Dallas in an open-top car, the president was gunned down as he drove through Dealey Plaza. Three shots were heard, with one fatally striking Kennedy in the head. Then-Vice President Lyndon B. Johnson was sworn in as president that same day aboard Air Force One.

Shortly after the attack, Lee Harvey Oswald, a former Marine who had lived in the Soviet Union and who had communist learnings, was arrested as the prime suspect. However, Oswald was assassinated two days later by Jack Ruby, a nightclub owner, while in police custody, further fueling conspiracy theories.

Kennedy's assassination left a deep scar on the American psyche. The official Warren Commission report concluded that Oswald acted alone, but many Americans have continued to doubt this official version. The assassination marked the end of the optimism that characterized the early 1960s and was seen as the beginning of an era of greater distrust of the government.

In political terms, Kennedy's assassination allowed his successor, Lyndon B. Johnson, to push through the civil rights legislation that JFK had proposed, as well as other important social reforms, such as the War on Poverty and the creation of programs like Medicare and Medicaid. However, Johnson's presidency was also marked by the escalation of the war in Vietnam, which led to greater polarization and division in American society.

Kennedy's legacy remains the subject of debate, but his assassination left an indelible mark on American history and the public perception of politics, marking the beginning of an era of greater cynicism and distrust in the country's institutions.

13. The assassination of Rafael Trujillo: The beginning of the end of a dictatorship

On May 30, 1961, dictator Rafael Leónidas Trujillo Molina, who ruled the Dominican Republic with an iron fist for more than three decades, was assassinated in an assassination attempt organized by a group of civilian and military conspirators. This assassination put an end to one of the most repressive and long-lasting regimes in Latin America. The political and social context surrounding Trujillo's assassination is key to understanding the reasons behind his death, as well as the internal and external tensions that ultimately precipitated his downfall.

Trujillo assumed power in 1930 following a coup d'état and quickly consolidated his control over all aspects of the Dominican Republic's political, economic, and social life. His government was characterized by a cult of personality, fierce repression of the opposition, and systematic use of violence to maintain power. Trujillo used intelligence services, such as the feared Military Intelligence Service (SIM), to spy on, imprison, torture, and assassinate his opponents.

Although Trujillo promoted economic modernization and carried out some infrastructure works, his regime was deeply marked by corruption, nepotism, and repression. He controlled most of the country's industries and businesses, enriching his family and a small circle of collaborators while most of the population lived in poverty.

One of the darkest episodes of his dictatorship was the Parsley Massacre in 1937 when he ordered the killing of between 15,000 and 30,000 Haitians on the border with Haiti. Trujillo, a fervent nationalist, used the discourse of "racial purity" to justify his policies against Haitians, who were brutally murdered to "Dominicanize" the border.

Despite his absolute control over the country, throughout the 1950s and early 1960s, discontent with the Trujillo regime grew both inside and outside the Dominican Republic. The dictatorial government brutally repressed any manifestation of dissent, but some sectors began to organize secretly to overthrow him.

The influence of the Catholic Church played an important role in the growing internal opposition. In 1960, the Dominican bishops, in a courageous action, issued a pastoral letter condemning the human rights violations committed by the regime. This stance of the Church, together with international pressure, weakened Trujillo's legitimacy and encouraged many of his internal enemies to look for ways to eliminate him.

In parallel, a group of young people and intellectuals began to organize clandestinely, inspired by the ideas of freedom and democracy that were spreading in Latin America and the Caribbean. These groups began to mobilize, creating networks of resistance and conspiracy.

In addition to growing internal opposition, the Trujillo regime was under strong international pressure, especially from the United States. During the Cold War, the Trujillo government had been seen as an ally in the fight against communism, and its anti-communist stance allowed it to maintain Washington's support. However, in the final years of his dictatorship, relations with the United States began to deteriorate.

One of the key factors in this change was the attempted assassination of Venezuelan President Rómulo Betancourt in 1960, orchestrated by Trujillo. This act of international aggression provoked condemnation from the international community and resulted in diplomatic and economic sanctions against the Dominican Republic. The Organization of American States (OAS) imposed an embargo on the country, which intensified Trujillo's isolation and further weakened his regime.

The John F. Kennedy administration in the United States also began to view Trujillo as a relic of the past and an obstacle to the expansion of democracy in the Western Hemisphere. Washington, concerned about the rise of communist movements in Latin America following the Cuban Revolution of 1959, no longer viewed Trujillo as a reliable ally, but as a dictator whose repression could foment popular rebellion and instability.

Growing internal discontent, coupled with international isolation, created ideal conditions for a group of conspirators to plan the assassination of Trujillo. This group was made up of middle-class figures, businessmen, and military officers who had lost confidence in the regime. Some of these conspirators had been loyal to Trujillo but had become disillusioned with his increasing authoritarianism and his inability to adapt to the new political times.

One of the most prominent leaders of the conspiracy was Antonio de la Maza, a former Trujillo associate whose family had been victims of the regime's repression. De la Maza, along with other conspirators such as Juan Tomás Díaz, Amado García Guerrero, and Salvador Estrella Sadhalá, carefully planned the assassination.

On the night of May 30, 1961, the conspirators ambushed Trujillo's car on the road to San Cristóbal, where the dictator often visited his mistress. Trujillo, traveling without an escort, was shot dead. Although the assassination was successful, the conspirators did not gain the immediate support they had hoped for for a general uprising against the regime.

Although Trujillo was removed, his regime did not collapse immediately. Trujillo's son, Ramfis Trujillo, returned to the country to try to maintain control, and for several weeks, repression intensified against those involved in the attack and their relatives. Many of the plotters were captured and brutally murdered.

However, Trujillo's death marked the beginning of the end of the dictatorship. The regime could not survive without its central figure, and international pressure, especially from the United States, helped accelerate the transition process. In November 1961, Ramfis and the Trujillo family left the country, and in 1962 the first democratic elections were held in the Dominican Republic in more than three decades. Juan Bosch, a prominent opponent of the regime, was elected president, marking the beginning of a process of democratization.

The assassination of Trujillo not only ended one of the longest-running and cruelest dictatorships in Latin America but also opened the door to the country's democratization, although the road to full democracy was long and full of challenges. Trujillo's assassination remains a milestone in the history of the Dominican Republic, remembered as the event that freed the country from more than 30 years of oppression.

14. The Assassination of Patrice Lumumba: Struggle for Congolese Independence

On January 17, 1961, Patrice Lumumba, the prime minister of the Democratic Republic of the Congo (DRC), was brutally assassinated in circumstances that reflect the complexity of late colonialism, ethnic tensions, and the growing conflict between Cold War powers. Lumumba, a nationalist leader and symbol of the African independence movement, was the victim of a plot involving both domestic and international interests, resulting in his tragic murder. The political and social context surrounding his death is crucial to understanding the causes and consequences of this assassination, which left a deep mark on African history.

Congo, under Belgian rule since the late 19th century, was one of the most brutally exploited colonial territories in Africa. During the reign of King Leopold II of Belgium, the Congo was treated as the personal property of the monarch, where millions of Congolese died due to forced labor and inhumane conditions in the extraction of rubber and other resources. Even after the Congo became an official colony of Belgium in 1908, Belgian colonial policies remained oppressive, with institutionalized racism and extreme economic exploitation.

By the mid-20th century, the push for independence in Africa was growing in strength, influenced by anti-colonial movements elsewhere in the world. In the Congo, Lumumba emerged as a key figure in the struggle for independence. He founded the Congolese National Movement (MNC) in 1958, a party that advocated national unity, full independence from Belgium, and an end to the ethnic division that the Belgians had deliberately fostered to maintain control.

On June 30, 1960, the Congo achieved its independence from Belgium, and Patrice Lumumba was elected prime minister of the new state. In his independence speech, Lumumba openly condemned the abuses of the Belgian colonial regime, which immediately strained relations with the former mother country. Despite initial euphoria, the young Congolese nation faced a series of crises almost immediately after its independence.

One of the main problems was the country's lack of preparation for self-government. Belgium had made little effort to educate or train the Congolese to govern their own country, and when they left, they left an institutional vacuum. Moreover, the Congo's resources, especially its vast mineral reserves, were coveted by foreign powers, which increased internal instability.

In July 1960, just weeks after independence, the mineral-rich province of Katanga, led by Moïse Tshombe, proclaimed its secession with the support of Belgian and Western interests. Katanga province was vital to the Congo's economy because of its wealth in copper and other minerals, and its secession weakened Lumumba's central government. Belgium, which still had significant economic interests in Congo, supported Tshombe in his struggle to maintain control of Katanga.

Lumumba's assassination must also be understood in the broader context of the Cold War, in which the two superpowers, the United States and the Soviet Union, competed for influence in the newly independent countries of Africa and Asia. Lumumba, with his nationalist approach and refusal to align himself exclusively with the West, was viewed with increasing suspicion by the United States and its allies.

Although Lumumba was not a communist, his willingness to accept aid from the Soviet Union during the Katanga crisis placed him in the crosshairs of Washington, which feared that the Congo would fall under Soviet influence. At the time, the United States was following the Eisenhower Doctrine, which viewed the spread of communism as a direct threat to its global interests. The Congo's natural resources, especially its uranium (used in the manufacture of nuclear weapons), were of great strategic importance.

The CIA became actively involved in efforts to weaken and eventually eliminate Lumumba. According to declassified documents, CIA Director Allen Dulles authorized his elimination shortly after his election as prime minister. In addition, Belgium, which still retained a strong influence in Congo, collaborated on plans to overthrow Lumumba, who posed a threat to its economic and political interests in the region.

As the situation in the Congo deteriorated, the president of the republic, Joseph Kasavubu, supported by the West, decided to dismiss Lumumba in September 1960, accusing him of mismanagement and links to communism. Lumumba, however, rejected this decision and continued to exercise power, leading the country into a state of political chaos.

Colonel Joseph Mobutu, who then led the army and would later become dictator of the Congo for decades, took advantage of the situation to carry out a military coup in September 1960. Mobutu, with the backing of the CIA and Belgium, arrested Lumumba and assumed control of the country. Although Mobutu initially handed power to Kasavubu, he remained a key figure in subsequent events.

Lumumba briefly managed to escape house arrest and tried to flee to the east of the country, where he hoped to reorganize his forces. However, he was captured by forces loyal to Mobutu and transferred to the breakaway province of Katanga, where he was imprisoned by the Tshombe regime.

On 17 January 1961, Lumumba was executed along with two of his associates, Maurice Mpolo and Joseph Okito, by firing squad in Katanga, under the supervision of Belgian officials and with the complicity of Western intelligence services. The bodies were dismembered and dissolved in acid, to erase any trace of their existence.

Lumumba's assassination shocked the world. In Africa, he was seen as a martyr in the fight against colonialism and oppression, while in the West, although some governments tried to distance themselves from the assassination, the involvement of the United States and Belgium was clear.

His death sparked a wave of protests and condemnation in Africa and other parts of the world. Lumumba's assassination not only deprived the Congo of a visionary leader but also marked the beginning of a long period of instability and violence in the country. The Democratic Republic of the Congo fell under the dictatorial control of Mobutu in 1965, who, with the backing of the West, ruled with corruption and repression for more than 30 years.

Patrice Lumumba remains a symbol of resistance against colonialism and neocolonial exploitation. His assassination reflected the international tensions of the Cold War and the internal struggles faced by many newly independent African nations. Despite his tragic death, Lumumba's legacy continues to inspire generations of Africans in their struggle for sovereignty, justice, and unity.

15. The assassination of Luis Carrero Blanco: A decisive blow to the Franco regime

On December 20, 1973, Luis Carrero Blanco, president of the Spanish government and right-hand man of dictator Francisco Franco, was assassinated in an attack perpetrated by the terrorist organization ETA (Euskadi Ta Askatasuna). This attack, which involved the detonation of a car bomb in the center of Madrid, marked a milestone in the recent history of Spain, not only because of the magnitude of the attack but also because of its political implications in the last years of the Franco regime. The assassination occurred in a context of great political and social tension, with a country facing both the oppression of a dictatorship and the growing discontent of nationalist sectors, opponents, and clandestine movements calling for democracy.

Carrero Blanco, a career soldier, was one of Francisco Franco's most trusted men. He had risen through the military and political hierarchy of the regime after the Spanish Civil War (1936-1939) and became one of the fundamental pillars of Francoism. His loyalty to Franco, his organizational ability, and his conservative profile ensured him a privileged position within the regime. In June 1973, Franco, already elderly and in poor health, was appointed president of the government, leaving him de facto in charge of the day-to-day affairs of the administration, while Franco retained the position of head of state.

Carrero Blanco was seen as the person in charge of ensuring the continuity of Francoism after Franco's death. He was a staunch defender of maintaining the authoritarian system and his role was crucial to the so-called "monarchical solution", that is, the restoration of the monarchy in the figure of Juan Carlos de Borbón under a regime controlled by Francoist forces, to prevent a transition to full democracy. This conservative vision clashed head-on with the democratic aspirations of a large part of Spanish society and of the opposition movements that were fighting for the end of the dictatorship.

At the beginning of the 1970s, Spain was at a crossroads. Although the Franco regime remained firm and authoritarian, social and political discontent was increasing. Opposition to Franco had been organized on various fronts: from communists and socialists, who operated clandestinely, to Basque and Catalan nationalists, who demanded greater freedom and autonomy. In factories and universities, workers' and student movements also expressed their rejection of the regime.

On an international level, Spain was increasingly isolated due to its dictatorial regime. While much of Western Europe was developing within a democratic and welfare framework, Spain remained under a repressive system that censored any form of dissent. This isolation affected the country both economically and politically. In this context, expectations for change were centered on the figure of Carrero Blanco, who represented the continuity of a system that many Spaniards wished to overcome.

Among the opposition movements to the Franco regime, one of the most significant and radical was ETA, a Basque nationalist group founded in 1959 to fight for the independence of the Basque Country and oppose the Franco regime. Initially, ETA adopted a more cultural and political stance, but as the regime remained inflexible and repression increased, the organization opted for more violent methods, including attacks and kidnappings. For ETA, Carrero Blanco symbolized the oppression of the Franco regime, not only against the Basque Country but against all of Spain.

Throughout the 1960s and early 1970s, ETA intensified its actions, which included attacks on government officials, police, and military personnel. In 1968, ETA carried out its first assassination with the murder of the head of the secret police in Guipúzcoa, Melitón Manzanas. This action was a turning point in ETA's evolution towards a more direct armed struggle against the regime.

The murder of Carrero Blanco was a meticulously planned and executed operation. For months, an ETA commando rented a flat on Claudio Coello Street in Madrid, close to the place where Carrero Blanco regularly attended mass. They dug a tunnel under the street, where they placed several explosives. On December 20, 1973, as Carrero Blanco's car passed by, the explosives detonated, causing the car to rise several meters into the air and land in an inner courtyard, instantly killing the Prime Minister.

The assassination of Carrero Blanco destabilized the Franco regime at a time when it was preparing its transition to a controlled monarchy. The disappearance of Franco's confidant left a power vacuum at a critical moment. Franco, devastated by the death of his main collaborator, was unable to find a replacement with the same authority and loyalty. Carlos Arias Navarro was appointed as the new Prime Minister, but his leadership did not have the same strength or the ability to ensure the continuity of the regime.

The attack also had a profound impact on the perception of the regime inside and outside Spain. ETA gained notoriety and demonstrated that the Franco regime, despite its repression, was not invulnerable. However, far from accelerating the fight for independence in the Basque Country, ETA's action increased repression in the Basque and Catalan regions, where the regime responded with arrests and executions of activists.

Internationally, the murder of Carrero Blanco was perceived as a decisive blow to the Franco regime, which from that moment began its final decline. Franco, elderly and increasingly weak, died two years later, in 1975, leaving Spain on the verge of a political transition that would culminate in the establishment of democracy and the 1978 Constitution.

16. The assassination of Park Chung-hee: When the hand meant to protect is the one doing the killing

The assassination of President Park Chung-hee on October 26, 1979, marked a turning point in the history of South Korea. Park, who had ruled the country with a firm hand since 1961, was assassinated by his intelligence chief, Kim Jae-gyu, amid rising political, economic, and social tensions. This event ended nearly two decades of his authoritarian rule, which, while it had driven unprecedented economic growth, had also repressed political and civil liberties.

Park Chung-hee came to power in South Korea through a military coup in 1961, at a time when the country was facing serious economic and political challenges. South Korea, devastated by the Korean War (1950-1953) and struggling to consolidate its national identity in the face of the constant threat from North Korea, was mired in poverty and chronic political turmoil. Park, a former army general, saw an opportunity to stabilize the country and lead it towards development.

Under his leadership, South Korea underwent an unprecedented economic transformation, known as the Miracle on the Han River. Park implemented a series of economic reforms aimed at industrial development, with a strong focus on exports and infrastructure modernization. The government provided a favorable environment for the growth of industrial conglomerates, known as chaebols (such as Samsung, Hyundai, and LG), which played a central role in the country's economic development. This growth led to a significant increase in the standard of living of South Koreans but also cemented centralized power under Park's control.

However, Park's economic success was accompanied by increasing political repression. In 1972, amid a climate of political instability and fears of internal and external threats, Park declared the Yushin Constitution, which gave him near-dictatorial powers. Under the Yushin regime, the president had complete control over the state apparatus, parliament, and judicial system. Repression of political dissidents, media censorship, and persecution of student and union activists became the norm.

As the 1970s progressed, political and social tensions in South Korea increased. While the country was experiencing rapid economic growth, Park's authoritarianism and lack of political freedoms generated discontent, especially among the emerging middle class, students, and workers. Student protests became increasingly frequent, demanding democratic reforms and an end to the Yushin regime.

Industrial relations also began to become strained, as many workers, especially in the industrial sector, felt exploited by the chaebols and harsh working conditions imposed in the name of economic development. Despite economic growth, social inequality and a lack of labor rights created fertile ground for social dissatisfaction.

On the international level, South Korea was at a crossroads. Although it maintained a firm alliance with the United States, which supported Park as an anti-communist bulwark in the region, Washington began to push for democratic reforms. At the same time, the Cold War and tensions with North Korea kept the country in a state of constant alert, which Park used as a justification for her authoritarian regime.

In 1979, internal tensions came to a head. In October, mass protests broke out in the city of Busan, which quickly spread to Masan and other areas of the country. The demonstrations, known as the Busan-Masan Protests, were led by students and workers demanding democratic reforms and Park's resignation. These protests represented a direct challenge to the government, and the regime's response was brutal, with martial law imposed and a heavy crackdown.

As the protests escalated, tensions within Park's inner circle also began to arise. Kim Jae-gyu, the director of the Korean Central Intelligence Agency (KCIA) and one of Park's closest aides, had deep differences with presidential security chief Cha Ji-chul, who supported increasingly repressive measures against protesters. Cha was seen as an extremist, and his influence over Park created internal tensions in the government.

Kim, on the other hand, believed that repressive policies would only make the situation worse and that a more moderate approach could save the country from a possible insurrection or military coup. He was frustrated by Cha's growing influence and Park's intransigence in reforming his government.

On October 26, 1979, during a dinner at the Safe House in Seoul, Kim Jae-gyu made a drastic decision. In a tense moment during the meal, Kim pulled out a pistol and fatally shot Park Chung-hee and her security chief, Cha Ji-chul. Park was killed instantly, ending 18 years of authoritarian rule.

Park's assassination shocked the nation and sparked an immediate crisis in the government. Kim was arrested shortly after the attack, and during his trial, he justified his actions as an attempt to save South Korea from a dictatorship that he claimed would lead the country to catastrophe. He claimed that his decision to kill Park was necessary to restore democracy and prevent civil war. However, many analysts believe that Kim also acted out of personal motives, given his frustration with Cha Ji-chul and the fact that his influence over Park had waned.

Park Chung-hee's assassination left a power vacuum in South Korea. Although the country's economy was still booming, political instability was evident. The government entered a chaotic transition phase, and South Korea was under martial law for several months. General Chun Doo-hwan eventually took control of a military coup in 1980, installing another authoritarian regime that would last until 1987.

However, Park's death also catalyzed the process of democratization in South Korea. Although the military dictatorship continued for a few more years, popular protests and growing social discontent eventually led to the democratic reforms of 1987, which marked the beginning of modern South Korea, a stable democracy with a robust economy.

The assassination of Kim Jae-gyu, while violent and dramatic, reflected the deep divisions within the regime and the exhaustion of a system that could no longer sustain itself in the context of a changing society. In time, South Korea would emerge as one of Asia's most vibrant democracies, and Park Chung-hee's assassination would be remembered as a pivotal moment in that difficult but inevitable process.

17. The assassination of Anwar Sadat: Religious hatred over peace

The assassination of Egyptian President Anwar Sadat on October 6, 1981, was a pivotal moment in the history of the Middle East and Egypt. His death occurred during a military parade in Cairo, when army soldiers, infiltrated by Islamist extremists, opened fire on the president. This assassination was deeply influenced by the social, political, and religious tensions that engulfed the country, as well as by Sadat's diplomatic decisions, particularly his historic signing of the Peace Treaty with Israel in 1979.

Anwar Sadat came to power in 1970 after the death of Gamal Abdel Nasser, the charismatic leader who had been the face of Pan-Arabism and Egyptian nationalism for almost two decades. Unlike Nasser, whose rule was marked by a foreign policy of confrontation with the West and Israel, Sadat presented himself as a leader willing to seek peace and liberalize the Egyptian economy.

His rule was initially characterized by an attempt to distance himself from Nasser's socialist policies and to establish a more pragmatic relationship with Western powers. One of Sadat's first moves was to expel Soviet advisers from the country, which was seen as a clear sign of rapprochement with the United States and other Western nations.

One of the key moments of Sadat's presidency was his leadership during the Yom Kippur War in 1973, a conflict in which Egypt and Syria launched a joint offensive against Israel to recapture territories lost in the 1967 Six-Day War. Although the conflict did not end in a decisive military victory, the war restored some Arab pride and allowed Sadat to position himself as a leader capable of challenging Israel and negotiating from a position of greater strength.

Sadat subsequently made the decision that would define his legacy: the pursuit of peace with Israel. After years of war between the two countries, Sadat shocked the world in 1977 when he visited Jerusalem and addressed the Israeli parliament, the Knesset, pleading for peace. This initiative culminated in the signing of the Camp David Accords in 1978, brokered by US President Jimmy Carter, and finally in the Egypt-Israel Peace Treaty in 1979.

For these efforts, Sadat was awarded the Nobel Peace Prize alongside Israeli Prime Minister Menachem Begin. However, this agreement was not well received in the Arab world. Egypt, which had historically been the leader of Arab nationalism, was repudiated by many Arab countries and the Arab League moved its headquarters from Cairo to Tunis as a sign of disapproval. Sadat was accused of betraying the Palestinian cause and breaking Arab unity.

While Sadat achieved international fame as a courageous leader and advocate of peace, he faced growing criticism at home. His opening to the West and economic liberalization policies, known as Infitah, failed to solve the deep economic problems affecting the population. The cost of living was rising, and the lower classes felt marginalized in a country where corruption and social inequality were rampant.

In addition, Sadat's economic reforms benefited elites and businessmen close to the government, while the middle and lower classes faced increasing hardship. In 1977, Egypt witnessed violent protests over rising food prices, after Sadat implemented a series of cuts to government subsidies as part of his economic liberalization agenda.

Social discontent came not only from economic sectors but also from the growing Islamist movement that saw Sadat's policies as a betrayal of Egypt's religious and national principles. Radical Islamists, many of whom had been repressed during Nasser's regime, began to gain ground during Sadat's presidency.

Although Sadat attempted to reconcile with Islamist groups in his early years, they began to view him as a traitor not only for his rapprochement with Israel but also for his close relationship with the United States. Sadat also allowed greater religious freedom, which paradoxically facilitated the growth of radical Islamism, particularly Egyptian Islamic Jihad, an extremist group that would be instrumental in his assassination.

Anti-Western and anti-Israel sentiment grew within these Islamist groups, who saw the signing of the peace treaty with Israel as an act of betrayal against the Umma (the Islamic community). In addition, Sadat was perceived as an increasingly authoritarian leader who repressed his critics through arrests and censorship.

In September 1981, just a month before his assassination, Sadat launched a massive crackdown, arresting more than 1,500 political opponents, including Islamists, communists, and liberal activists. This crackdown only increased tensions, and radical Islamists began planning their revenge.

On October 6, 1981, during a military parade commemorating Egypt's victory in the Yom Kippur War, President Anwar Sadat was assassinated. A group of soldiers, led by Lieutenant Khalid Islambouli, a member of the Egyptian Islamic Jihad, infiltrated the parade. Armed with rifles and grenades, they disrupted the official ceremony and opened fire on Sadat, who was killed instantly along with several military officers.

The attack was the result of a careful plan orchestrated by Islamic Jihad and other extremist groups who considered Sadat a traitor to the Arab and Muslim cause. Islambouli and his accomplices, who acted with coldness and precision, had no intention of fleeing; they believed their action was an act of martyrdom in defense of Islam.

Sadat's assassination left Egypt in a state of political uncertainty. He was succeeded by his vice president, Hosni Mubarak, who would rule the country for nearly three decades in an authoritarian style like Sadat's, but with greater emphasis on repressing Islamist movements.

Sadat's assassination also deepened divisions in the Arab and Muslim world. Although the peace treaty between Egypt and Israel survived, tensions between Arab countries, Islamist factions, and Western states persisted.

Sadat was remembered as a leader who changed the course of Egyptian and Middle Eastern history, risking his life for peace. However, his decision to break with decades of hostility towards Israel and its alignment with the West cost him his life. The assassination of Sadat marked not only the end of his life but also the beginning of a new era of instability and violence in Egypt, which still faces the challenges posed by Islamist radicalism and internal tensions.

18. The assassination of Ronald Reagan: The curious connection with Hollywood

The assassination of US President Ronald Reagan on March 30, 1981, was an event that shook both the nation and the world. Reagan, who had assumed the presidency just months earlier, miraculously survived an attack in which the attacker fired six shots in a few seconds. Although it was an incident with profound political and social implications, the attack was essentially the result of an isolated act carried out by a psychologically disturbed individual, rather than a direct reflection of the political tensions of the time.

Ronald Reagan assumed the presidency of the United States on January 20, 1981, after a resounding victory over the outgoing Democratic president, Jimmy Carter. Reagan, a former film actor and governor of California, had built his political platform on a message of strengthening the economy through a policy of cutting taxes and decreasing government regulation. This approach became known as Reaganomics and promised to reduce government spending while boosting economic growth.

On the international level, Reagan came to power at a time of high tension in the Cold War between the United States and the Soviet Union. Reagan was a staunch critic of communism and had promised to take a tougher stance towards Moscow, unlike Carter's more diplomatic approach. Reagan advocated the need for a sharp increase in the military budget, which would be part of his strategy to contain Soviet expansion.

Furthermore, Reagan's term coincided with a complex social context. The United States was still recovering from the economic disaster of the 1970s, with high rates of inflation and unemployment. There was also increasing political polarization, with many citizens fearful of the expansion of government power and concerned about economic security and Soviet influence in the world. Although these tensions were evident, they were not the direct cause of the assassination attempt against Reagan.

The attacker, John Hinckley Jr., did not act for political or ideological reasons. His motivation arose from his obsession with actress Jodie Foster. Hinckley had seen the film Taxi Driver (1976), starring Robert De Niro, in which the main character attempts to assassinate a politician to impress a woman. Inspired by this plot, Hinckley developed an unhealthy obsession with Foster and came to believe that performing a dramatic and violent act, such as the assassination of a president, would make him stand out in the eyes of the actress.

Over several months, Hinckley tried various ways to contact Foster, who was then a student at Yale University, but when he received no response, he decided to plan an assassination attempt on the president. Before attacking Reagan, Hinckley had followed Jimmy Carter on several trips, although he never found the opportunity to get close to the outgoing president. When Reagan took office, Hinckley made him his target.

On March 30, 1981, Ronald Reagan was leaving the Washington Hilton Hotel in Washington, D.C., after giving a speech to a group of labor leaders. As he walked to his limousine, accompanied by Secret Service agents and other officials, John Hinckley Jr. emerged from the crowd and fired six shots from a .22-caliber Röhm RG-14 revolver.

One of the shots ricocheted off the armored limousine and hit Reagan in the chest, puncturing a lung and leaving it just inches from his heart. Fortunately, the quick action of Secret Service agents and the medical team allowed Reagan to arrive in time at George Washington University Hospital, where he underwent emergency surgery. Reagan made a full recovery, and his ability to cope with the attack won him great public sympathy.

In addition to Reagan, three other people were injured in the attack:

James Brady, the White House press secretary, was hit in the head and suffered permanent brain injuries that left him partially paralyzed.

Timothy McCarthy, a Secret Service agent, was wounded in the abdomen while protecting the president.

Thomas Delahanty, a Washington police officer, was wounded in the neck.

The attack on Ronald Reagan had no clear political motivation, but the political and social consequences were profound. First, Reagan's figure was notably strengthened. His image of strength, sense of humor, and optimism during his recovery, including his famous comment before being operated on, "I hope you're all Republicans," contributed to his growing popularity. This allowed his political agenda to gain momentum, helping Congress pass several of his economic reforms.

In the security realm, the attack led to a reevaluation of presidential security protocols. Even though the Secret Service had implemented rigorous measures, the attack demonstrated that risks were still high at public events. After the attack, presidential protection practices were strengthened, and additional measures were taken to prevent future assassination attempts.

The attack also had an impact on gun control. Although not immediate, the attack renewed the debate over access to firearms in the United States. James Brady, the press secretary injured in the attack, became a fervent advocate for gun control. Together with his wife Sarah, they advocated stricter legislation, eventually leading to the passage of the Brady Bill in 1993, which established a waiting period and background checks for the purchase of firearms.

John Hinckley Jr. was arrested immediately after the attack and put on trial. In 1982, he was found not guilty due to mental illness. This verdict sparked a great deal of public debate, as many people believed that, despite his mental state, Hinckley should have been sentenced to prison. As a result of this verdict, Congress passed stricter laws regarding mental health defenses in criminal trials.

Hinckley spent decades in custody at a psychiatric hospital. In 2016, he was released under strict conditions, although he continued to be monitored by authorities.

19. The Assassination of Pope John Paul II: Religion and Politics amid the Cold War

On May 13, 1981, Pope John Paul II was the victim of an assassination attempt in St. Peter's Square at the Vatican, an attack that shocked the world. As he waved to the crowd from his popemobile, a Turkish man named Mehmet Ali Ağca shot him four times, seriously wounding him. The pontiff, wounded in the abdomen and hands, was rushed to hospital, where he underwent emergency surgery that saved his life. This assassination attempt had profound religious as well as political implications and occurred in a global context marked by the Cold War, the ideological struggle between the capitalist West and the communist bloc.

John Paul II, born Karol Józef Wojtyła in Poland in 1920, was elected Pope in 1978. His election was historic, as he became the first non-Italian pontiff in more than 450 years. In addition, he came from Poland, a country under communist control, which made his election have a strong impact in the context of the Cold War. From the beginning of his papacy, John Paul II took an active stance in defense of human rights and religious freedom, which made him a staunch critic of the communist regime in Eastern Europe.

His support for opposition movements, especially the Solidarity trade union in Poland, made him a key figure in the peaceful resistance to communism. Solidarity, led by Lech Wałęsa, challenged Soviet control and sought improvements in workers' rights, being one of the main actors in the eventual fall of communism in Eastern Europe.

John Paul II's opposition to communism, as well as his support for human rights and civil liberties, positioned him as a highly influential figure both inside and outside Europe. However, they also made him a target for those who saw his role as a threat to communist regimes.

In 1981, the world was at the height of the Cold War, a confrontation between the superpowers of the United States and the Soviet Union, which divided the world between rival ideologies: capitalism and communism. The influence of the Catholic Church and Pope John Paul II in particular, who advocated freedom and human rights in communist countries, was seen as a threat to the stability of communist regimes, especially in Eastern Europe.

Poland, John Paul II's home country, was at the center of this tension. The Solidarity movement, which had gained strength in the late 1970s and early 1980s, had become a symbol of resistance to Soviet control. The Pope's tacit support for the movement was evident, and his visit to Poland in 1979 had been an inspiration to millions seeking to free themselves from the communist yoke.

The Pope's role in destabilizing communist regimes in Eastern Europe led to theories linking the assassination attempt to the Soviet bloc's secret services, in particular the KGB and the intelligence services of Bulgaria, a country closely aligned with Moscow. Although not fully confirmed, some historians and experts believe the attack was part of a broader plot to silence John Paul II, whose influence represented a challenge to communism.

Mehmet Ali Ağca, the man who attempted to assassinate the Pope, was a member of a Turkish ultra-nationalist group called the Grey Wolves, known for their right-wing extremism and opposition to communist ideologies. Before the attack, Ağca had already been convicted of the murder of Turkish journalist Abdi İpekçi in 1979 but had managed to escape from prison.

Ağca had repeatedly declared his hatred of the West and the Catholic Church and claimed that the Pope represented a symbol of "Westernism" that should be eliminated. However, Ağca's exact motives for attacking John Paul II remain a matter of debate. Following his arrest, he offered various conflicting accounts of his motivation, further fuelling theories that he may have acted under the influence of secret services from communist countries.

During his trial, Ağca claimed that he had been recruited by Bulgarian intelligence, prompting Italian authorities to investigate a possible communist plot. However, although several Bulgarian officials were arrested and tried, no conclusive evidence was found linking the Soviet bloc to the attack.

On 13 May 1981, John Paul II was touring St Peter's Square in the Vatican, greeting the faithful from his popemobile, as was his custom. Mehmet Ali Ağca, who was in the crowd, fired four shots from close range, seriously wounding the Pope in the abdomen, left hand, and right arm. Despite his injuries, John Paul II was quickly taken to Gemelli Hospital, where he underwent emergency surgery.

The news of the attack shook the world. For several days, the pontiff's life was in danger, but thanks to medical intervention, he survived. In the years that followed, John Paul II considered his survival a miracle, linking the fact that the attack occurred on the anniversary of the apparition of Our Lady of Fatima, on May 13. He even went so far as to visit Ağca in prison in 1983, in a gesture of forgiveness that astonished the world.

In political terms, the attack failed in diminishing the Pope's influence in world politics. His stance against communism grew stronger, and he continued to be a key supporter of the Solidarity movement in Poland, which would ultimately play a crucial role in the fall of communism in Eastern Europe towards the end of the 1980s.

John Paul II's ability to forgive his attacker and his continued fight for peace and freedom after the attack cemented him as one of the most influential figures of the 20th century.

20. The assassination of Indira Gandhi: Operation Blue Star, the key to the conflict

On October 31, 1984, the Prime Minister of India, Indira Gandhi, was assassinated by two of her bodyguards at her official residence in New Delhi. This assassination was the result of a series of political, religious, and social tensions that had been building up for years around the conflict between the Indian central government and the Sikh community, particularly after the controversial military operation known as Operation Blue Star. Gandhi's assassination was a high point of the sectarian violence that was tearing India apart, and her death sparked a wave of riots and retaliation across the country.

Indira Gandhi, daughter of India's first prime minister, Jawaharlal Nehru, was an influential political figure who ruled India in two periods (1966-1977 and 1980-1984). During her tenure, she promoted nationalist and modernizing policies, but she also accumulated a great deal of power, becoming an authoritarian figure in certain respects. Her rule was marked by important achievements, such as the 1971 war that led to the creation of Bangladesh, and by controversial episodes such as the Emergency between 1975 and 1977, when she suspended civil rights and imprisoned political opponents.

However, Indira Gandhi's tenure was also plagued by internal challenges, including growing conflicts between religious communities in India, particularly with the Sikh community, a minority but powerful group in the north of the country, especially in the state of Punjab.

The Sikh community, which has its spiritual seat at the Golden Temple in Amritsar, Punjab, has been facing tensions with the central government for decades. The Sikhs, who constituted a significant minority in India, were a community that enjoyed a strong cultural and religious identity. During the 1980s, some radical elements within the Sikh community began to advocate the creation of an independent state called Khalistan, which sparked tensions between the Sikhs and the Indian government.

Radical Sikh leader Jarnail Singh Bhindranwale became the main proponent of this separatist movement, and under his leadership, the Golden Temple became a stronghold of armed Sikh militants. Bhindranwale had been gaining strength in his demand for greater autonomy for Punjab and for the Sikh community, which brought him into open confrontation with the government of Indira Gandhi.

In 1984, tensions between the Indian government and the Sikh separatists reached a peak when Indira Gandhi ordered a military operation to dislodge the militants from the Golden Temple, resulting in Operation Blue Star. This operation, which took place in June 1984, consisted of a military assault on the most sacred Sikh shrine, and although Bhindranwale was killed along with many of his followers, the raid provoked a strong reaction in the Sikh community.

The use of military force inside the Golden Temple was seen by many Sikhs as a desecration of their most sacred site, and images of Indian soldiers entering the temple with guns and tanks angered Sikhs around the world. Although Indira Gandhi's government justified the operation as a necessary measure to stamp out terrorism, the repercussions were profound, as it polarized the nation and further alienated the Sikh community.

Tensions between the Sikh community and the Indian government escalated rapidly after Operation Blue Star. Indira Gandhi, despite warnings from her advisors, decided to continue to keep Sikh members in her personal security detail, which was seen as an act of trust or defiance. However, this decision proved fatal.

On October 31, 1984, two of her Sikh bodyguards, Beant Singh and Satwant Singh, ambushed her as she was on her way to a televised interview at her residence. Beant Singh shot her three times with his revolver, and then Satwant Singh fired several shots with his machine gun. Indira Gandhi was rushed to the hospital but died shortly after due to the severity of her injuries.

Gandhi's assassination was a direct result of the deep wounds caused by Operation Blue Star and the resentment of the Sikh community over the invasion of the Golden Temple. The assassins, motivated by a sense of revenge for what they considered an affront to their religion, carried out one of the most significant assassinations of the 20th century.

The assassination of Indira Gandhi sparked a wave of anti-Sikh violence across the country, especially in New Delhi. For several days, thousands of Sikhs were killed by angry mobs, while thousands of Sikh businesses and homes were looted and burned. It has often been alleged that the Congress Party, which led the government, was involved in instigating and allowing the riots, further aggravating sectarian tensions.

These reprisals created a deep scar in the relationship between the Sikh community and the Indian state. At the national level, Indira Gandhi's death also led to a transition in power. Her son, Rajiv Gandhi, took over as prime minister shortly after her assassination and continued to lead India through a period of political and social instability.

The assassination of Gandhi was not only an act of personal revenge but also a reflection of the political and religious tension of a time when the Indian state was struggling to maintain unity in the face of complex internal challenges.

21. The assassination of Olof Palme: An assassination in a peaceful country

On 28 February 1986, Swedish Prime Minister Olof Palme was shot dead in central Stockholm as he walked with his wife, Lisbet Palme, after leaving a movie. The assassination shocked not only Sweden but the entire world, due to Palme's public profile and the fact that his murder remained unsolved for decades. The political and social context surrounding this assassination is deeply rooted in Olof Palme's charismatic leader and the global and national tensions surrounding him.

Olof Palme was one of Sweden's most prominent political figures during the 20th century. Born into a wealthy family in 1927, Palme became leader of the Swedish Social Democratic Party and served as Prime Minister twice, from 1969 to 1976 and from 1982 until his assassination in 1986. During his tenure, he promoted social welfare policies and was a strong advocate of human rights, peace, and Swedish neutrality.

Internationally, Palme was an influential voice against colonialism, apartheid in South Africa, and the Vietnam War, making him a respected but also controversial figure. He was one of the few European leaders to openly criticize both the United States and the Soviet Union, to keep Sweden a neutral nation amid the Cold War.

Palme supported various liberation movements in Third World countries and championed causes such as Namibian independence, the Palestinian struggle, and opposition to the dictatorial regime of Augusto Pinochet in Chile. This stance put him in the crosshairs of various groups, both domestic and international, who saw him as a threat to their interests.

Domestically, Sweden during the 1980s was a prosperous country, with a social welfare system that was the envy of the world. However, it also faced growing problems. Despite its economic and political stability, there was increasing tension around issues such as immigration, crime, and political radicalization.

The country was beginning to experience the first signs of social and political fractures. On the one hand, the social welfare policies that Palme advocated began to be criticized by the political right that advocated more liberal reforms in the economy. On the other hand, the more conservative sectors and certain extremist groups in Sweden began to see Palme as a threat to the country's traditional values, partly due to his strong support for international left-wing movements and his criticism of right-wing dictatorships.

On the evening of February 28, 1986, Olof Palme decided to go out without security escorts, as he usually did, to go to the cinema with his wife. After the screening, the two were walking down a central street in Stockholm when a man approached from behind and shot Palme at point-blank range. The prime minister died almost instantly. Lisbet Palme was also wounded but survived the attack.

The murder caused instant shock in Sweden. The country, which had been known for its low crime rate and social peace, was shaken by the first assassination in its modern history. However, despite the shock and the efforts of the authorities, the investigation into the crime stalled, and for years the killer could not be identified with certainty.

The murder of Olof Palme has been the subject of numerous conspiracy theories due to the lack of conclusive evidence. Over the decades, various theories have emerged, some based on his political stances and others on more local theories.

<u>Swedish right-wing groups and extremists</u>: One of the most persistent theories is that the murder was committed by an individual or group linked to the Swedish far right, who saw Palme as a threat due to his progressive policies and support for international left-wing movements.

<u>International groups</u>: Palme's anti-apartheid stances in South Africa and his staunch opposition to US

intervention in Vietnam made him a potential target for foreign organizations. Some pointed to the South African secret services as possible perpetrators, as Palme was a fierce critic of the apartheid regime.

<u>Kurdish connection:</u> At one point in the investigation, Swedish police explored the theory that the murder was linked to a Kurdish separatist group called the PKK (Kurdistan Workers' Party). However, this line of inquiry was eventually discredited.

<u>Christer Pettersson:</u> In 1989, a man named Christer Pettersson was arrested and convicted of Palme's murder. Pettersson was a common criminal with a history of drug abuse. However, the conviction was overturned in 1989 due to a lack of solid evidence, and although Pettersson remained a prime suspect, his guilt was never conclusively confirmed.

Stig Engström and the final resolution: In 2020, the Swedish prosecution service formally closed the case of the murder of Olof Palme, identifying Stig Engström, a graphic designer and witness to the crime, as the prime suspect. Engström, also known as "the Skandia man," had been mentioned in the previous investigation but had not been seriously considered as a suspect. Engström died in 2000, leading authorities to conclude the investigation without being able to prosecute the culprit.

The murder of Olof Palme left an indelible mark on Sweden and international politics. Domestically, Sweden was faced with the reality that, despite its stability and peace, it was not immune to political violence. The assassination sparked a period of national introspection, questioning the nature of power and the security of public leaders in an open society.

On the international stage, Palme's death deprived the world of one of the strongest voices for neutrality, peace, and human rights. His legacy has been remembered as that of a courageous leader who stood by his convictions to the end, despite internal and external pressures.

Palme's assassination was a tragic conclusion to a life dedicated to public service, but his legacy has endured as a symbol of politics based on moral and ethical principles in a world divided by ideological conflicts.

22. The assassination of Thomas Sankara: The "African Che Guevara"

On October 15, 1987, Burkina Faso's revolutionary leader Thomas Sankara was assassinated in a coup d'état orchestrated by his close associates, including Blaise Compaoré, who would later take power. Sankara's assassination was not only the end of a four-year mandate, but the collapse of a revolutionary project that attempted to profoundly transform the political, economic, and social structure of Burkina Faso. The political and social context that led to this tragic event was marked by the struggle between Sankara's progressive forces and internal and external pressures seeking to maintain the status quo in West Africa.

Thomas Sankara, born in 1949, was a young military officer who stood out for his charisma and his radical approach to the social and political transformation of Burkina Faso, then known as Upper Volta. Sankara came to power in 1983 following a coup d'état that, ironically, was led by his friend and comrade-in-arms, Blaise Compaoré. From the start of his term, Sankara set out to profoundly change the course of the nation, renaming it Burkina Faso, meaning "the land of upright men," to break away from the French colonial legacy.

Sankara promoted a pan-African revolution based on self-sufficiency, social justice, gender equality, and economic independence. Rather than relying on foreign aid, Sankara advocated collective labor and agricultural development as the foundations for the country's growth. His radical approach earned him the appreciation of many inside and outside Africa but also attracted the attention and opposition of those who felt threatened by his policies.

During his four years in power, Sankara pushed through a series of social and economic reforms that transformed Burkina Faso. Among his major achievements were:

<u>Land redistribution:</u> Sankara encouraged peasants to farm self-sufficiently and dramatically reduced the country's dependence on foreign food aid.

<u>Vaccination campaigns:</u> Under his leadership, Burkina Faso became one of the few African countries to achieve mass vaccination campaigns, successfully reducing infant mortality.

Empowerment of women: Sankara promoted gender equality by banning female genital mutilation, forced marriage, and polygamy. He also encouraged women to actively participate in public and political life.

Fighting corruption: Sankara implemented drastic measures to reduce corruption, cut back on the privileges of public officials, and led a modest lifestyle, rejecting luxuries that characterized other African leaders.

Rejection of foreign debt: Sankara was a fierce critic of foreign debt and the influence of Western powers in Africa, going so far as to say at the 1987 Organization of African Unity (OAU) Summit that "we must not pay the debt. The debt cannot be repaid because if we do not, our children and grandchildren will have to do it."

However, these reforms also faced opposition from various sectors both at home and internationally. Domestically, his rapid and radical approach generated tensions with sectors of the military, the economic elite, and traditional leaders, who felt threatened by the loss of privileges.

Sankara became an uncomfortable figure for many foreign powers. His anti-imperialist stance, his call for African self-sufficiency, and his criticism of Western influence on the continent earned him enemies on several fronts. France, the former colonial power, viewed Sankara's leadership with disfavor, as it feared that his ideas would spread to other Francophone nations in West Africa, affecting its geopolitical and economic interests in the region.

In addition, Sankara's close relationship with Libya and its leader Muammar Gaddafi caused concern among Western powers and some African leaders, as Gaddafi was seen as a destabilizing figure in international politics.

At home, Sankara also faced growing tensions within his power circle. His radical vision and aggressive reforms began to alienate some factions within the military, especially those who had supported his rise to power but did not share his revolutionary approach.

One of the main conspirators was his friend and comrade-in-arms Blaise Compaoré, who was initially integral to the revolution but later began to distance himself from Sankara. Compaoré, influenced by foreign interests and internal elites who felt displaced, began to perceive Sankara as an obstacle to his political ambitions. The relationship between the two deteriorated rapidly.

On 15 October 1987, Justice Minister Blaise Compaoré, with the help of the French government of François Mitterrand, led a military coup against Sankara in Ouagadougou, the country's capital. He was assassinated along with several of his closest collaborators. His body was dismembered and buried in an unmarked grave, and his widow and children fled the country. A week before his execution he famously said: "Although revolutionaries, as individuals, can be killed, their ideas can never be killed."

The assassination of Thomas Sankara marked the end of a revolutionary era in Burkina Faso and was seen as a blow to the pan-African and anti-imperialist movements in Africa. Blaise Compaoré, who consolidated his position in power, maintained a government that was more aligned with Western powers and halted many of the radical reforms that Sankara had implemented.

However, Sankara's figure has endured as a symbol of struggle and resistance for many Africans and people around the world. Despite his brief tenure, Sankara left a profound legacy in African history, especially in his call for self-reliance, social justice, and gender equality. His vision of an Africa free from the shackles of foreign debt and dependency continues to resonate in political and social movements across the continent.

Decades after his assassination, Sankara's name continues to evoke respect and admiration. In 2016, the government of Burkina Faso, following the fall of Blaise Compaoré, decided to exhume Sankara's remains and conduct an official inquiry into his death. In 2021, Blaise Compaoré was tried in absentia for his role in Sankara's assassination, marking a step towards historic justice.

Today, Thomas Sankara is remembered as the "African Che Guevara," an inspiring figure whose legacy of fighting oppression, colonialism, and economic exploitation lives on in the collective memory of Burkina Faso and beyond.

23. The assassination of Mohamed Boudiaf: Amid the political storm

On June 29, 1992, Mohamed Boudiaf, the president of Algeria, was assassinated while giving a public speech in the city of Annaba. His assassination occurred just six months after assuming the presidency, at a time of great political and social unrest in Algeria. This assassination reflected the political crisis that the country was going through, characterized by the rise of radical Islamism, internal struggles within the military power, and the growing polarization between reformist and conservative sectors. To understand the context of Boudiaf's assassination, it is necessary to analyze the complex political situation in Algeria at the time, marked by decades of authoritarianism, social tensions, and an impending civil war.

Since its independence from France in 1962, Algeria has been governed by the National Liberation Front (FLN), the political party that had led the war of independence. For three decades, the FLN maintained an authoritarian regime with strong state control over the economy and society. Despite having achieved some initial stability, the FLN regime was eroded by corruption, clientelism, and a lack of democratic freedoms, which generated discontent among broad sectors of the population, especially among the youth.

In the 1980s, Algeria was facing a severe economic crisis, exacerbated by falling oil prices, leading to rising unemployment, poverty, and inequality. In this context, political Islamism began to gain ground as an alternative to the secular and authoritarian FLN regime. The Islamic Salvation Front (FIS), founded in

1989, became the main opposition force, gaining massive support among the popular classes, who saw Islamism as a form of protest government corruption and repression.

In 1991, the FIS won a landslide victory in legislative elections, alarming the government and the military. Faced with the prospect of an Islamist party taking control of the country, the Algerian military intervened and annulled the election results, sparking a violent uprising by FIS supporters and triggering a civil war known as the Black Decade.

Mohamed Boudiaf was one of the founders of the FLN and played a key role in Algeria's struggle for independence. However, after independence, he was ostracized by his fellow revolutionaries and went into exile in Morocco, where he lived for almost three decades, removed from Algerian politics.

In 1992, to save the country from total collapse, the Algerian military decided to bring Boudiaf back as a consensus figure to lead a political transition. A High Council of State, a military junta that would assume power after the suspension of elections, was formed and Boudiaf was appointed president of this institution. His mission was to restore order and implement political and economic reforms that would calm growing popular discontent.

Boudiaf accepted the mission in the hope of implementing democratic reforms and eradicating the corruption that had marked the FLN regime. Upon his return, he attempted to dismantle the old power structures and confront the military and political factions that controlled the country. However, his proposal for rapid change and his challenge to the established power provoked resistance within the military and political apparatus itself.

On June 29, 1992, while giving a speech at a cultural center in Annaba, Mohamed Boudiaf was shot dead by one of his bodyguards, Lieutenant Lambarek Boumaarafi, an officer in the Presidential Guard. The assassination occurred in front of television cameras, shocking the country and the world.

The motivations for Boudiaf's murder have been the subject of speculation and controversy ever since. Boumaarafi was immediately arrested and claimed that he had acted alone for personal reasons. However, many maintain that the murder was the result of a broader conspiracy within the armed forces and sections of the FLN who saw Boudiaf as a threat to their interests. The fact that Boudiaf attempted to reform the system and directly confront corruption and military power made him enemies both in the military and in the political establishment.

Boudiaf's assassination reflected the deep divisions within Algerian society and the state. At the time, Algeria was in the grip of a spiral of violence pitting Islamists against the military. The FIS, which Boudiaf had attempted to politically neutralize, had become radicalized after the annulment of the elections and had begun to carry out armed attacks against the government.

Boudiaf, although he returned as a reformer, was faced with an extremely fragile situation: radicalized

Islamists on one side and the corrupt military leadership on the other. His attempt to navigate between these two opposing forces and reform the system from within became unsustainable. The inability to consolidate a strong political base, coupled with the rejection of the sectors that controlled power, led to his assassination.

The assassination of Mohamed Boudiaf left a leadership vacuum in Algeria at a critical moment. His assassination further exacerbated tensions and contributed to the intensification of the armed conflict between the government and the Islamists. The Black Decade, which had already begun before his assassination, escalated, causing the deaths of more than 200,000 people in a brutal civil war that lasted until the early 2000s.

The military regime that had orchestrated Boudiaf's rise to power was consolidated after his death, and the reforms he had attempted to implement were put on hold. For years, the military government continued to fight Islamist factions in a war that devastated the country in both human and economic terms.

Despite his brief tenure, Mohamed Boudiaf is remembered in Algeria as a leader who tried to change the course of the country in one of the darkest moments of its history. His assassination is seen as a reminder of the forces operating behind power in Algeria and the difficulty of implementing deep political changes in a context of instability and violence.

Today, Boudiaf is regarded by many Algerians as a martyr to the reformist cause and his figure has been rehabilitated in public discourse, especially after the brutality of the civil war and the subsequent stabilization of the country. His assassination, however, remains a matter of debate, with many still questioning the exact circumstances surrounding his death and the actors behind the plot.

24. The assassination of Juvénal Habyarimana: the beginning of the largest African genocide

On April 6, 1994, Rwandan President Juvénal Habyarimana was assassinated when the plane he was traveling on was shot down near Kigali, the country's capital. This attack not only ended the president's life but also triggered one of the most brutal genocides of the 20th century, where approximately 800,000 people, mostly of the Tutsi ethnic group, were killed in just 100 days. To understand the reasons behind Habyarimana's assassination and the devastating consequences that followed, it is essential to analyze the political and social context of Rwanda at the time, marked by deep ethnic divisions, regional tensions, and the collapse of an authoritarian system.

Since its independence from Belgium in 1962, Rwanda has been marked by ethnic conflict between the Hutu majority and the Tutsi minority. During the colonial period, the Belgians favored the Tutsis, giving them positions of administrative power, which created resentment among the Hutus. After independence, a series of uprisings and conflicts led to the establishment of a Hutu-dominated regime, which displaced the Tutsis from the power structures and consolidated their control over the state.

Juvénal Habyarimana, an ethnic Hutu military officer, came to power in 1973 through a coup d'état, overthrowing then-President Grégoire Kayibanda, also an ethnic Hutu. During his rule, Habyarimana established an authoritarian regime under the National Republican Movement for Democracy and Development (MRND), which controlled virtually all aspects of political life in Rwanda. His regime favored the ethnic Hutus, and the Tutsis were politically and socially marginalized, while many of them were forced to flee to neighboring countries, such as Uganda, where they began to organize themselves militarily.

For the next two decades, Rwanda remained under one-party rule, with strong control over the media and state institutions. However, as the country's economy deteriorated and ethnic tensions rose, Habyarimana's regime began to face increasing challenges.

In exile, the Tutsi community formed the Rwandan Patriotic Front (RPF), a political-military group that aimed to overthrow the Hutu regime and secure the return of Tutsi refugees to Rwanda. The RPF, led by Paul Kagame, launched its first offensive against Habyarimana's government in 1990 from Uganda, triggering a civil war that would last until 1994. The RPF invasion exacerbated ethnic tensions and led the Habyarimana regime to tighten its control and intensify propaganda against the Tutsis, portraying them as an existential threat to the nation.

The Habyarimana government, with the support of radical Hutu sectors known as Hutu Power, began to arm and train paramilitary militias, such as the Interahamwe, which would be responsible for many of the crimes committed during the genocide. At the same time, peace negotiations between the government and the RPF, driven by international pressure, led to the signing of the Arusha Accords in 1993, which provided for the establishment of a transitional government that would include both Hutus and Tutsis.

However, the more radical sectors of the Hutu government viewed the Arusha Accords as a betrayal and feared that the return of the Tutsis to power would jeopardize their control over the state. These political and ethnic tensions, combined with mistrust of peace processes, created a climate of fear and hatred, paving the way for the massive violence that would erupt in 1994.

On the night of April 6, 1994, the plane carrying Juvénal Habyarimana and Burundi President Cyprien Ntaryamira was shot down by missiles near Kigali airport. The two presidents were returning from a summit in Tanzania where they had discussed the implementation of the Arusha Accords. The authorship of the attack remains a matter of controversy to this day.

Some point to the Rwandan Patriotic Front (RPF) as the culprit, arguing that the RPF had an interest in eliminating Habyarimana to hasten its military victory and consolidate power. However, other researchers and experts maintain that it was Hutu extremists who shot down the plane, seeking to provoke a crisis that would allow them to take full control of the government and carry out the planned massacre of the Tutsis. This theory is since the Hutu militias were already prepared to act at the time of the attack, suggesting prior planning.

The assassination of Habyarimana was the spark that ignited a wave of brutal violence. Within hours, the Interahamwe militias, supported by the army and the police, began attacking the Tutsi population and moderate Hutus who opposed extremism. For the next three months, Rwanda was the scene of a systematic genocide, in which Tutsi men, women, and children were killed in their homes, schools, and churches. The violence was not limited to executions with firearms; many of the killings were carried out with machetes and other crude weapons, reflecting the level of hatred and dehumanization that had been cultivated by years of anti-Tutsi propaganda.

Meanwhile, the Rwandan Patriotic Front (RPF) continued to advance militarily and managed to take control of Kigali in July 1994, ending the genocide. Paul Kagame, the leader of the RPF, assumed power in Rwanda, and a new government was established, although the country was devastated both physically and socially.

The assassination of Juvénal Habyarimana is remembered as the catalyst for one of the darkest episodes in contemporary history. The violence that followed the assassination unleashed a humanitarian catastrophe of epic proportions and left a deep mark on the collective memory of Rwanda and the world. The international community was criticized for its inaction during the genocide, as UN forces in Rwanda were unable to stop the violence.

Since then, Rwanda has attempted to rebuild itself under the leadership of Paul Kagame, who has been praised by some for his role in stabilizing the country, although his government has also been criticized for its authoritarianism and lack of political freedoms. The scars of the genocide remain present in Rwandan society, and the country continues to grapple with the aftermath of collective trauma, the search for justice, and reconciliation between Hutus and Tutsis.

25. The assassination of Yitzhak Rabin: When hatred and intolerance are in the air.

The assassination of Yitzhak Rabin on November 4, 1995, marked a turning point in Israel's political history and the complex dynamics of the Arab-Israeli conflict. Rabin, then prime minister of Israel, was shot dead by Yigal Amir, a Jewish extremist opposed to the Oslo Accords, in an attack that deeply shocked both Israeli society and the international community.

Yitzhak Rabin, a general turned statesman, played a key role in establishing Israel and defending it in multiple wars. However, it was his pragmatic vision for peace that led him to seek an agreement with the Palestinians, a shift that was seen by many as a betrayal of traditional Zionist principles.

In 1993, Rabin signed the Oslo Accords with Palestinian leader Yasser Arafat, to end the Israeli-Palestinian conflict. These accords represented the first serious attempt to create a framework for coexistence between Israel and a future Palestinian state. They included mutual recognition between the Palestine Liberation Organization (PLO) and Israel, as well as the establishment of Palestinian self-government in the Gaza Strip and parts of the West Bank, territories Israel had occupied since the Six-Day War in 1967.

Although the Oslo Accords were greeted with hope by many Israelis and the international community, they also generated strong opposition in conservative and right-wing Israeli quarters. Many viewed any territorial concessions as an existential threat to the security of the Jewish state. Jewish settlers in the occupied territories felt betrayed by Rabin's government, as the accords involved the possibility of dismantling settlements and ceding control over parts of what they considered "promised land."

As the peace process progressed, Israeli society became increasingly polarized. Right-wing sectors, led by the Likud party and figures such as Benjamin Netanyahu, denounced the Oslo Accords as a surrender of Israel's security to its enemies. Mass demonstrations against the peace process took place, some of them openly violent in tone and inflammatory rhetoric.

Religious and ultra-nationalist groups, who believed strongly in the vindication of "Greater Israel", saw Rabin as a traitor who endangered Israel's survival by making concessions to the Palestinians. This rhetoric was fueled by political opposition leaders and religious figures who constantly attacked Rabin in public speeches and in the media. Demonstrations were held in which he was compared to dictators such as Hitler, and images of Rabin in a Nazi uniform were circulated. This level of demonization contributed to a climate of hatred and verbal violence that would eventually have deadly consequences.

On November 4, 1995, Yitzhak Rabin was taking part in a pro-peace rally in Tel Aviv, which had gathered tens of thousands of people under the slogan "Yes to peace, no to violence." At the end of the rally, as Rabin was leaving the stage, he was shot at point-blank range by Yigal Amir, a 25-year-old law student who was fiercely opposed to the Oslo Accords and who acted alone.

Amir, who belonged to the religious Zionist movement, believed that the Oslo Accords were a betrayal of the fundamental principles of Judaism and that Rabin, by signing them, had violated Jewish religious law. Amir justified himself by invoking the concept of din rodef, a religious interpretation that, in extreme cases, allows for the killing of someone who is endangering the lives of other Jews. In his mind, Rabin was condemning Israeli settlers and citizens to death by giving away land to Palestinians.

The assassination shocked the nation. Rabin was rushed to hospital but died shortly after from his wounds. The bullet that ended his life not only cut short the leadership of a man committed to peace but also dealt a severe blow to the peace process, which never fully recovered from his death.

Yitzhak Rabin's death was a national trauma for Israel. Tens of thousands of Israelis attended his funeral, and world leaders, including US President Bill Clinton, traveled to pay tribute to a man who had worked tirelessly to achieve peace in a region scarred by decades of conflict. In Israel, the assassination was seen as a symbol of the deep divisions within society, and the political class was forced to reflect on the level of polarization that had allowed such violence to take place.

Rabin's assassination sparked a wave of condemnation against extremists who fomented hatred and violence. Many pointed to the violent discourse and extremist rhetoric that dominated the political environment as having played a crucial role in creating an environment in which a young religious fanatic felt justified in assassinating the prime minister. However, some sectors saw in Amir a hero who had, by his action, prevented Israel from making unacceptable concessions in its struggle for security.

Rabin's assassination also had a profound impact on the peace process. After his death, his successor, Shimon Peres, continued peace efforts, but the process quickly stalled due to new episodes of violence, including suicide bombings by Palestinian groups such as Hamas. In the 1996 elections, Benjamin Netanyahu, leader of the Likud and a fierce opponent of the Oslo Accords, won the election, marking the end of the push for a peace agreement on the terms put forward by Rabin.

Today, the assassination of Yitzhak Rabin is still remembered as a critical moment in Israel's history. Every year, a day of remembrance is held in his honor, where his legacy and the impact of his assassination on Israeli politics are reflected. Although the peace process never again reached the level of progress it had achieved during Rabin's tenure, his commitment to a two-state solution and reconciliation with the Palestinians remains a reference point in the debate over Israel's future.

Rabin's assassination was a devastating reminder of the consequences of political polarization and extremism, and his legacy remains a warning about the dangers of allowing hatred and intolerance to prevail in public discourse.

26. The assassination of Zoran Đinđić: The fight against organized crime and corruption

The assassination of Zoran Đinđić, the Prime Minister of Serbia, on 12 March 2003, deeply shook the country and reflected the political and social tensions that persisted after the fall of the regime of Slobodan Milošević. Đinđić was a key figure in Serbia's democratization process and its reintegration into the international community after the conflicts of the 1990s in the Balkans. However, his efforts to reform the country and confront the corrupt and criminal power structures that had emerged during the war made him a target for those who feared losing their position and influence.

Zoran Đinđić was a key player in the democratic movement that ended the era of Slobodan Milošević, the authoritarian leader who had dominated Serbian politics for more than a decade. In 2000, Milošević was overthrown following a series of mass protests known as the Bulldozer Revolution, led in part by Đinđić and his party, the Democratic Party. This event marked the end of a regime that had led Serbia into a series of devastating conflicts, international sanctions, and diplomatic isolation.

Once in power, Đinđić set about implementing a series of political, economic, and judicial reforms aimed at modernizing Serbia and transforming it into a democratic, functioning state with a market economy. He was also one of the first Serbian leaders to recognize the need for reconciliation with the international community and with Western European countries, something that Milošević had vehemently rejected.

However, these reforms met resistance in various quarters of the country. Power structures that had been strengthened during the war, including elements of the army, police, and security services, were not willing to lose their influence. These institutions were deeply intertwined with criminal networks that thrived during the 1990s through smuggling, arms trafficking, and paramilitary activities.

One of Đinđić's greatest challenges was his fight against organized crime and corruption, which had penetrated the highest levels of the state. After

Milošević's fall, it became clear that many of the powerful figures in Serbia had built fortunes and power networks through illicit activities, and any attempt at reform was bound to meet with fierce opposition from these quarters.

Đinđić took decisive steps to weaken these networks, including the arrest of key figures of the former regime and the extradition of Slobodan Milošević to the International Criminal Tribunal for the former Yugoslavia in The Hague in 2001. This extradition was particularly controversial and caused outrage among nationalist sectors and Milošević's allies, who viewed Đinđić as a traitor who was handing his countrymen over to foreign hands.

In addition, Đinđić pushed through a series of judicial reforms to target criminal gangs that controlled much of the economy and security in Serbia. These measures included the creation of special police units and the strengthening of courts to prosecute leaders of organized crime. This made him a direct enemy of powerful mafia groups that had thrived during the chaos of the war years.

One of the most powerful and feared groups during the Balkan war was the "Arkan Tigers", a paramilitary unit founded by Željko Ražnatović, known as Arkan. This group was linked to numerous war crimes and had profited greatly from criminal activities during the conflicts of the 1990s. Although Arkan was killed in 2000, his criminal networks remained active, and many of its members became part of the security forces and organized crime after the war.

In particular, the criminal group "Special Operations Unit" (Jedinica za specijalne operacije, JSO), known as the "Red Berets", was a paramilitary unit that had participated in military operations during the war and subsequently became involved in criminal activities. This unit was deeply involved in smuggling and drug trafficking, and many of its members viewed Đinđić's reforms as a threat to their power and influence.

On 12 March 2003, while on his way to a meeting at the government building in Belgrade, Zoran Đinđić was shot by a sniper. The assassin, Zvezdan Jovanović, a member of the JSO, fired from a nearby building, killing the prime minister instantly. Jovanović later stated that he had murdered because he considered Đinđić a traitor to Serbia's interests and that his government was handing the country over to foreign powers.

The attack was not an isolated act, but part of a broader conspiracy within the circles of organized crime and former members of the security apparatus that had thrived during the Milošević regime. These sectors saw Đinđić as an obstacle to maintaining their power and control over state institutions, and his murder was an attempt to protect their interests.

The murder of Zoran Đinđić unleashed a wave of shock in Serbia. Thousands of people took to the streets to pay tribute to a leader who, despite the criticism he had received for his policies, represented the hope for a modern and democratic Serbia. Đinđić's death symbolized the great challenge of transforming a country devastated by years of war and corruption.

Following the assassination, the Serbian government launched Operation Sabre, a massive campaign against organized crime that resulted in hundreds of arrests, including prominent crime figures and members of the former security apparatus. Although the operation was a success in terms of dismantling part of the criminal networks, Đinđić's legacy as a reformer was cut short.

In the years since his death, Serbia has continued to struggle to find a balance between its turbulent past and its future as part of Europe. Đinđić's assassination remains a reminder of the dangers faced by those seeking to reform deeply divided societies, and of the forces that resist change in defense of vested interests.

Today, Zoran Đinđić is remembered as a visionary leader who sought to guide Serbia into a new era of democracy, modernity, and peace. His assassination underlined the deep resistance he faced in trying to dismantle the criminal and authoritarian structures that had flourished under the Milošević regime. Despite his tragic death, his legacy lives on in Serbia's collective memory and his effort to integrate the country into the European community is a path that remains relevant in Serbian politics today.

27. The assassination of Mahmoud Ahmadinejad: Ethnic and regional tensions. The Ahvazi problem

On 4 August 2005, Mahmoud Ahmadinejad, who had recently assumed the presidency of Iran, was the target of an assassination attempt during a visit to the city of Ahvaz in the southwest of the country. This attack was unsuccessful in its aim of assassinating the president, but it reflected the internal tensions that marked Iranian politics at the time, as well as problems related to ethnic identity and regional conflicts. Ahmadinejad, an ultra-conservative leader, faced not only the challenge of governing a country with deep internal divisions but also the pressure of international geopolitical tensions.

Mahmoud Ahmadinejad was elected president of Iran in June 2005 after a campaign that portrayed him as a defender of Islamic revolutionary values and a man of the people, in contrast to the moderate technocrats who had ruled Iran in previous decades. His victory represented a return to the more conservative principles of the 1979 Islamic Revolution, raising concerns both at home and abroad.

Ahmadinejad was a staunch defender of Iran's theocracy and the supreme leadership of Ayatollah Ali Khamenei. His anti-Western stance and belligerent rhetoric, especially against Israel and the United States, began to raise international tensions soon after he assumed the presidency. Within Iran, however, Ahmadinejad also faced a growing divide among political elites: on the one hand, radical conservatives who supported his theocratic vision for the country, and on the other, reformists who sought greater openness and modernization of the Iranian economy and society.

The assassination of Ahmadinejad occurred in Ahvaz, a city in the province of Khuzestan, near the border with Iraq. This region is rich in oil, making it a strategic part of the country, but it is also an area of ethnic tensions, as much of the population is of Arab origin, a minority in Iran. Over the years, the Arab population of Khuzestan had expressed discontent with the policies of the central government, alleging discrimination and economic marginalization. These tensions were exacerbated by political repression and a lack of adequate representation in the government.

Discontent in Ahvaz and its surroundings was not new. In 2005, a series of explosions and bombings in the region, blamed on Arab separatists, had highlighted ethnic tensions in the area. Iranian Arabs, who represent a small minority in the country, had suffered for years under policies they considered discriminatory and had tried, on several occasions, to gain greater autonomy. These separatist movements, although not widespread, had become a source of instability in a region key to Iran's economy due to its significant oil reserves.

The attack in question occurred when a convoy accompanying Ahmadinejad was attacked in Ahvaz. Although the exact details of the incident were unclear, it was reported that a grenade was thrown towards the presidential convoy, killing one person and wounding two others. Ahmadinejad emerged unharmed from the attack. The Iranian government was quick to downplay the incident, suggesting that the bombing had been an attempt at sabotage by opponents of the government or separatist elements in the region.

The attack reflected the difficulties Ahmadinejad faced in his attempt to maintain control over a country that was not only politically divided but also had deep ethnic and regional divisions. The discontent in Ahvaz was just one of many sources of internal instability that would mark his tenure.

The attack was quickly attributed to Arab separatists in the Khuzestan region, although some speculated that it could also have been the work of rival political factions within Iran itself. In a country like Iran, where tensions between different political groups have often led to violence, it was not impossible that Ahmadinejad's political enemies, both among the reformists and the more pragmatic conservatives, could be involved.

The Iranian regime used the attack to justify further repression in the Khuzestan region and other areas with minority populations, which in turn exacerbated tensions. In addition, the incident heightened the perception that the country was under constant threat, which strengthened Ahmadinejad's standing among his more conservative supporters, who saw him as a strong leader willing to confront internal and external challenges.

The assassination of Ahmadinejad occurred at a time when tensions between Iran and the West were rapidly escalating. His election as president marked a shift toward a more confrontational foreign policy, particularly about Iran's nuclear program.

Ahmadinejad took a defiant stance in the face of US and European demands that Iran halt its uranium enrichment, making him a controversial figure in international politics.

Moreover, his incendiary rhetoric against Israel and his denial of the Holocaust in public speeches attracted international condemnation and helped to further isolate Iran. At home, this stance strengthened Ahmadinejad among the more radical sectors of the Iranian establishment, who saw him as a defender of sovereignty and national interests against foreign powers.

28. The assassination attempts against Fidel Castro: Political and social context behind the multiple assassination attempts

Fidel Castro, the Cuban revolutionary leader who ruled the island from 1959 to 2008, survived countless assassination attempts throughout his life, many of which were orchestrated by the CIA, anti-Castro organizations, and political dissidents. Although exact numbers vary, it is estimated that more than 600 attempts were made in his life, making him one of the most attacked leaders in modern history. The motives behind these attacks were deeply rooted in the political, social, and geopolitical context surrounding Cuba during the Cold War.

Fidel Castro came to power in Cuba after leading the Cuban Revolution that overthrew dictator Fulgencio

Batista in 1959. The new revolutionary government, which promised social justice, equality, and the eradication of imperialism, quickly nationalized major industries and expropriated private property, much of which belonged to American businessmen and companies. This unleashed a series of conflicts with the United States, which until then had maintained considerable economic and political control over the island.

The deterioration of relations between Cuba and the United States was immediate. In 1961, the failed Bay of Pigs invasion, organized by the CIA and executed by Cuban exiles, marked a point of no return in the tensions between the two countries. This invasion, and Castro's growing support for the Soviet Union, consolidated Cuba as a key point in the ideological struggle of the Cold War. In this context, eliminating Fidel Castro became a strategic priority for the US government, which saw him as a direct threat to its influence in the Western Hemisphere.

The conflict between the United States and Cuba escalated rapidly, and the CIA, together with Cuban exile groups, began planning various methods to assassinate Fidel Castro. Throughout the 1960s and 1970s, assassination attempts against Castro were as numerous as they were varied. From explosives hidden in cigarettes, poison pills, and diving suits infected with fungus, to sniper attacks, the methods used in the attempts reflected the US obsession with eliminating him.

One of the most famous attempts was Operation Mongoose, a secret plan implemented under the John

F. Kennedy administration in 1961 after the failure of the Bay of Pigs. This program included economic sabotage, political destabilization, and of course, the assassination of Castro. The CIA worked closely with the Cuban American mafia and exiles to carry out these plans, but none were successful.

Castro, however, was aware of the CIA's efforts to eliminate him. In many public speeches, Castro mocked the failed attempts and cultivated an image of invulnerability, which only increased his prestige among his followers and allies, both inside and outside Cuba.

Assassination attempts against Castro came not only from outside Cuba but also from within, with the collaboration of anti-Castro groups. These groups, composed of dissidents and exiles, were supported and financed in many cases by the United States and other countries that saw in them the hope of a regime change on the island.

Within Cuba, these counterrevolutionary opposition movements had a limited, but significant, presence. Since coming to power, Castro had implemented a series of repressive measures to consolidate his control over the country. The purge of dissidents, censorship of the press, and total control of the state apparatus allowed him to minimize the influence of his internal enemies, but the threat remained latent. Several assassination attempts were orchestrated by figures within the same revolutionary circle, but the strict security measures and hierarchical structure of the government made it difficult for these attempts to progress.

For much of his term, Castro had the support of the Soviet Union, which saw him as a crucial ally on the American continent. The alliance between the USSR and Cuba was a constant source of tension between the Western and Communist blocs. Following the missile crisis in 1962, when the world was on the brink of nuclear war due to the presence of Soviet missiles in Cuba, Castro's figure was consolidated as an icon of resistance against the United States.

The Soviet Union, through its intelligence services, played an important role in protecting Castro. With the KGB collaborating with Cuban security agencies, Fidel Castro was one of the most closely watched leaders in the world. The Cuban intelligence system became extremely efficient at neutralizing threats and anticipating attacks, which contributed to Castro's survival in the face of so many assassination attempts.

Ironically, the continuous assassination attempts against Fidel Castro reinforced his image both inside and outside Cuba. For his followers, both on the island and in other countries, Castro represented resistance against imperialism and foreign intervention. The failed attempts to eliminate him only served to consolidate his reputation as an unbeatable leader. In his speeches, Castro often mocked the US's inability to kill him, further increasing his "legendary" status within the revolutionary movement.

Internationally, Castro became a figure of inspiration for other leftist movements in Latin America and elsewhere in the world, who saw in his survival proof of the ability of oppressed peoples to resist imperialist power. So, although none of these attempts were successful, each one formed part of the legacy of a leader who, despite efforts to remove him, remained in power for nearly five decades, becoming one of the longest-lived and most polarizing figures in 20th-century political history.

29. The assassination of Benazir Bhutto: Political tensions, religious extremism and the fight for democracy

The assassination of Benazir Bhutto on December 27, 2007, marked a key moment in the history of Pakistan, a country embroiled in political tensions, religious extremism, and the fight for democracy. Bhutto, the first woman to lead a Muslim country, was a symbol of hope for millions of Pakistanis. Her death, the result of a suicide bombing during an election rally in Rawalpindi, shocked the world and left a void in Pakistani politics. This tragic event was not only a personal attack on Bhutto, but also a reflection of the chaos and deep divisions that defined Pakistan at the time.

Benazir Bhutto came from an influential political family. Her father, Zulfikar Ali Bhutto, was both Prime Minister and President of Pakistan, and she served as Prime Minister twice, from 1988 to 1990 and from 1993 to 1996. However, both terms ended abruptly due to allegations of corruption and her forced exile. During this time, Pakistan witnessed increasing military control, under leaders such as General Pervez Musharraf, who seized power following a coup in 1999.

In 2007, Benazir Bhutto returned to Pakistan after several years in exile, as part of a deal between her and the Musharraf regime, brokered by the United States and the United Kingdom. This agreement sought to stabilize the country amid growing threats from radical Islamist groups, sectarian tensions, and international pressure to restore democracy. Musharraf, under pressure from both home and abroad, allowed Bhutto to return in the hope that her presence would calm the political situation and lend a veneer of legitimacy to elections scheduled for January 2008.

Bhutto's return was, however, extremely controversial. While many saw her as a force for change and modernization, other sections of the country, including Islamic extremists and figures within the government perceived her as a threat. Her pro-Western style and stance in favor of fighting radical extremism attracted the ire of groups such as the Taliban and Al-Qaeda, who saw her return as a Western attempt to impose a foreign agenda on Pakistan.

One of the most important factors behind Benazir Bhutto's assassination was the growing religious extremism in Pakistan. Throughout the 1990s and 2000s, Pakistan had become an epicenter for radical Islamist groups. The Taliban, which controlled significant parts of Afghanistan, maintained close ties with militant groups in Pakistan, such as Lashkar-e-Taiba and Jaish-e-Mohammed. These groups found refuge in Pakistan's tribal areas and were supported by sections of the Pakistani military and intelligence apparatus.

Following the September 11, 2001, attacks and the US invasion of Afghanistan, the situation in Pakistan deteriorated further. The Musharraf government, under pressure from the US, began to act against some of these groups, albeit inconsistently. This led to further radicalization of Islamist militants, who viewed the Musharraf government and politicians like Bhutto as traitors collaborating with the West in the so-called "war on terror".

Benazir Bhutto was seen as a direct threat by these groups. In several speeches, Bhutto had promised to crack down on Islamist militants and reform the tribal areas, making her a prime target for the Taliban and other extremists. Furthermore, her stance in favor of women's rights and democracy made her unpopular among the more conservative sections of Pakistani society, who rejected her modernizing agenda.

Bhutto's assassination came amid a climate of increasing political violence in Pakistan. The 2008 elections were scheduled to be a decisive moment for the country, as they were expected to mark the end of Musharraf's military dictatorship and the return to democracy. However, the country was in chaos. Suicide attacks, sectarian clashes, and military operations in tribal areas raised fears that the elections would be disrupted by violence.

The attack that killed Bhutto was not the first attempt to end her life. On 18 October 2007, just hours after her triumphant return to Pakistan, a suicide attack in

Karachi on a motorcade accompanying her killed more than 130 people. Although Bhutto emerged unscathed from the attack, the attack was a clear signal that her life was in danger. Yet, despite the risks, Bhutto continued her election campaign, declaring that she would not be intimidated by terrorism.

Pakistan's growing political instability, the fragility of Musharraf's government, and divisions within the security forces created a perfect breeding ground for the final attack. Bhutto was assassinated as she left a rally in Rawalpindi when a suicide bomber shot her and then detonated a bomb, killing more than 20 people in the process. Her death was a devastating blow to the country and plunged Pakistan into an even greater crisis.

The assassination of Benazir Bhutto had profound repercussions both in Pakistan and internationally. Her death left her party, the Pakistan People's Party (PPP), without its most charismatic leader and sparked a wave of protests and riots across the country. His assassination was condemned internationally by world leaders who viewed the attack as an act of terrorism aimed at destabilizing Pakistan and preventing its transition to democracy.

In Pakistan, Bhutto's assassination not only exacerbated political tensions but also deepened social and religious divisions. The country was at a crossroads, with Islamist extremists rising in power and fighting for control of state institutions. Musharraf, weakened by growing political opposition and international pressure, eventually resigned in 2008.

Bhutto's death also symbolized the failure of Pakistan's democratic transition and underlined the continuing danger facing political leaders in the country. Despite her tragic end, Benazir Bhutto remains remembered as an iconic figure in the fight for democracy in the Muslim world. Her legacy lives on in Pakistani politics, where her family, including her son Bilawal Bhutto Zardari, has sought to uphold her vision of a democratic and modern Pakistan.

30. The assassination of Muammar Gaddafi: The end of Africa's longest-serving dictator

October 20, 2011, marked the end of one of Africa's most repressive dictators: Muammar Gaddafi. After more than 40 years in power, the Libyan leader was captured and killed in the streets of Sirte by rebel forces, culminating in a period of intense civil conflict that led to the fall of his regime. This event not only marked the end of an era in Libya but also left profound repercussions in the region and globally.

Muammar Gaddafi assumed power in Libya in 1969 following a military coup that overthrew King Idris. During his tenure, Libya became an autocratic state under his control. Although he pushed through social and economic reforms, Gaddafi's regime was also notable for its brutal repression of dissent, corruption, and arbitrary wielding of power. In the years leading up to its fall, Libya began to experience growing internal tensions, stemming from popular discontent over the lack of political and economic freedoms.

The uprising that would lead to the collapse of the Gaddafi regime took place in the context of the Arab Spring, a series of protests that shook several countries in the Middle East and North Africa in 2011. Inspired by the movements that had overthrown the leaders of Tunisia and Egypt, Libyans began demonstrating in February 2011. The protests, initially peaceful, were violently suppressed by Gaddafi's forces, which quickly escalated into a civil war.

The confrontation between the rebels and forces loyal to Gaddafi attracted the attention of the international community. In the face of the atrocities committed by the regime, the United Nations Security Council passed Resolution 1973 in March 2011, authorizing the use of force to protect civilians. NATO's intervention was key to the development of the conflict, as it significantly weakened Gaddafi's army, which had managed to maintain its control over Tripoli and other strategic areas of the country, through airstrikes.

Gaddafi's government, which at one point seemed immovable, began to crumble as the rebels, with NATO support, advanced towards the capital. In August 2011, Tripoli fell to the insurgents, and Gaddafi was forced to flee to his hometown, Sirte, where he continued to resist until October.

On 20 October 2011, rebel forces managed to surround and capture Muammar Gaddafi on the outskirts of Sirte. His convoy was reportedly attacked by a NATO airstrike, forcing the Libyan leader to take refuge in a sewer along with some of his bodyguards. Shortly afterward, he was captured by rebel fighters. Images of Gaddafi being brutally abused and murdered by his captors were broadcast around the world. His body was flown to Misurata, where it was put on public display before being buried at a secret location in the desert.

The main motive behind Gaddafi's capture and killing was the collapse of his authoritarian regime and the rebels' desire to end decades of repression. During his rule, Gaddafi imposed absolute control over the country's institutions, stifling any opposition attempts. In addition, his erratic behavior in international politics, including his backing of terrorist groups and his strained relationship with Western powers, had turned Libya into a pariah state for many years.

The violent suppression of protests in 2011 was the spark that ignited the civil war, but the roots of the conflict lay in decades of abuse and marginalization of much of the Libyan population. Tribal and regional differences also played a role, with Gaddafi's power concentrated in Tripoli and areas in the west, while the east of the country, where the revolt began, had historically been marginalized.

The assassination of Muammar Gaddafi did not bring peace to Libya but rather triggered a prolonged period of chaos and violence. Without strong central leadership and with numerous armed factions vying for power, the country spiraled into instability that, more than a decade later, remains unresolved.

Libya was divided into multiple regions controlled by rival militias, leading to a prolonged civil war and intervention by foreign powers. The lack of a strong central government allowed the rise of extremist groups such as the Islamic State, which took advantage of the power vacuum to establish themselves in the country. In addition, Libya became a key point for human trafficking and arms smuggling in the Mediterranean, aggravating the migration crisis in Europe.

Internationally, Gaddafi's death and NATO's intervention in Libya caused divisions. While some regarded Gaddafi's overthrow as a victory for human rights and freedom, others argued that the Western intervention left the country in chaos. Criticism intensified over time, as the conflict in Libya had negative repercussions for the stability of the entire Sahel region and North Africa.

———————✝———————

Other books by the author Phillips Tahuer that you will find on this platform:

- The greatest conspiracy theories

- Great robberies in history

- Famous murderers - the evil side of the mind-

- Lives in captivity - Stories of real kidnappings-

- Agents, informants, and traitors - the world of espionage-

- Pirates of the 21st century

- Tragic loves

- 30 curiosities of World War II

- Dark experiments on humans

- Real-life heroes

- Powerful men in modern history

- Valentine's Day stories

- Lessons in Practical Psychology

- Deserters

- Attacks and assassinations